Cricut Project Ideas

How to Master Cricut and Create Original Project Ideas through Illustrations and Examples. A Guide for Beginners to Start Making Your First Project or Develop Your Abilities

Jessie Crafts

This book may contain advices, opinions and statements from various information providers. It does not represent or endorse the accuracy or reliability of the suggestions, opinions, declarations or other information provided by any information provider, any reader or any other person or entity. Trust in any advice, opinion, statement or other information will also be at the risk and expense of the reader. Neither the owner nor the author will be responsible to the reader or any other person for any inaccuracy, error, omission, interruption, elimination, defect, alteration or use of any content in this document, or for its timeliness or integrity.

Table of Contents

What is Cricut Machine?

The Cricut is a cutting machine. This, at least, is the correct term. However, it does not in the least describe the infinite potential of this machine. I own the Cricut Maker, currently the best machine in the series. With the Cricut Maker you can do just about anything: cut different materials, custom t-shirts, sewing projects, postcards, birthday invitations, banners, creative lamps, stickers, bracelets, embossed creations, custom blackboards, mugs and glasses, cut out letters or images for scrapbooking, and much, much more.

What you can do using Cricut

- Create stickers to stick in your car in your favorite items
- Create your own stencils for painting
- Create custom labels
- Personalize pillows, shirts, sweatshirts, tablecloths
- Produce an endless variety of Christmas ornaments
- Personalize glasses and mugs
- Engrave the plexiglass

- Make your own wall decals
- Create shapes from linden or balsa wood
- Create decals
- Making DIY slates
- Party banner
- Invitations for birthday
- Sewing projects
- Shapes for scrapbooking
- Leather items (diaries, bracelets, etc.)
- Puzzle

There are several different models, and the items that come with each machine vary from one to another. But there are some things that come universally with all machines.

Each machine comes with:

- A Cricut cutter
- One fine point blade and one premium blade cover
- A 12 × 12 inch "LightGrip" cutting mat.
- A USB cable
- A power adapter
- A welcome guide for easy setup
- A free trial membership for Cricut Access

- Access to 25 free projects ready to go
- Materials for a practice project.

Some models come with more elements, such as different blades, scoring wheels, or a special pen for writing.

The Cricut Machine is a plotter that can cut various materials and write / draw on them, it can also perforate them (create those tear lines typical of cinema tickets, so to speak), engrave them (for example Plexiglas and aluminum), create reliefs (such as in the case of embossing, even if in this house it is actually a debossing) or even folding lines (very useful if you make cards, tickets, boxes, etc.).

The machine will do one or the other depending on the accessory (blade, tip or pen) that we are using. This machine is the Rolls Royce of cutting machines. And for good reason! Imagine any media up to 3mm thick, the machine will cut it with ten times the power of the Cricut Explore and its other competitors. What made me fall for this machine is the possibility of cutting leather.

The Cricut machine can cut cardboard, balsa, vinyl, flex, burlap (!)... And FABRIC. Yes! You read that right fabric! And not just cotton! Not all kinds of fabric imaginable! In the Design Space you can find all kinds of fabrics: velvet, jersey, silk, lace! In all, the Maker cuts around 100 different materials up to

3mm thick. Another important feature of the Maker: you can write with it!

Whatever the type of material we want to work with the maker (paper, wood, jeans ...), we will have to introduce it in the machine after making it adhere on special reusable mats , mats that are equipped with a more or less resistant layer of glue : if we are using paper we will use a mat with a layer of not very resistant glue, if instead we are using wood we will use a mat with a much more powerful layer of glue.

The Cricut machine has a double carriage allowing two operations to be carried out in a single pass. It is thus possible to draw (or use the "scoring tool "to make folds) and cut at the same time.

Basic Material for Cricut Machine

The Cricut Explore and Cricut Maker machines can cut all kinds of materials and we've added a long list of pre-programmed settings to Design Space to give you great flexibility when working with different materials for your projects. You can choose from these pre-programmed settings or even create your own!

Select a platform below for step-by-step instructions on using, creating and modifying or deleting custom material settings.

1. Log into Design Space and create / open a project.
2. Make sure your Cricut Maker or Cricut Explore machine is turned on and connected to your computer.
3. Go to the project preview screen.
4. If you have a Cricut Explore machine, make sure your Smart Set dial is set to Custom. Select Browse All Materials.

Cricut Design Space Options

- In **Templates** you can choose between several elements, arranged in categories, prepared for you to use as a reference base to place your designs at the correct size. They will not be saved in your project.
- **Projects:** you can find in addition to your projects that are saved in the cloud, complete works ready to cut or sketch, you have some free for you to try.
- **Images:** You have hundreds of resources ready to cut or print and cut. Many are free.
- **Text: you** just have to write what you want and select the font and size.
- **Shapes:** you can choose some basic to use in your projects.

Tools & Accessories

The Cutout Tool

This tool is useful for many things, mainly to cut one part in another.

To understand its principle, we are going to take a kitchen tool: the cookie cutter

When you make your small cookie dough you take your cookie cutter in the shape you want and you press it on the dough, the result is a shape identical to the cookie cutter and a hole in negative compared to your cookie cutter.

In the Space design, it's the same, for example, you have a rectangle, you take another shape that you "press on" and you get the cookie cutter, the cut-out shape and the negative shape on the part below.

First of all :

- I advise you to ungroup the elements before cutting them
- You can only cut two pieces at the same time. If you select 3, the Cutout tool will be automatically grayed out.

The functions of the cutting tool

1. Cut out (this one we would not have believed)
2. Crop (and this is mainly how I use this tool)
3. The cutouts off the mat!

1. The cutting punch

To show this function I insert a Heart on my canvas as well as a smiling Cricut cricket! If your Cricut locust is below the heart, click "arrange" and then "send forward". We can now place the Cricut locust where we want it.

Once you are happy with your arrangement, select the two pieces and click on cut at the bottom right.

And here you are with 3 pieces as you can see in the layers panel.

Let's go back to the image of the cookie cutter: you have the cookie cutter, the piece it cut and the negative piece.

2. Crop (and this is mainly how I use this tool)

For some reason (If anyone at Cricut reads me I'm interested in knowing more!) There is no Crop tool in the Design Space except when uploading an image.

The trick is to use the cutting tool to achieve our ends

For the example, I take the image Succulents (# M1AABF32 Rad & Happy).

I only want the first and the fifth pot. I insert a square in the canvas

I unlock the measurements to make it a rectangle and I place it to hide the other pots.

I select both parts and cut them via the cutout tool. On the layers panel, I see that several parts have been created after our cutting. I keep only the last one and delete the rest (right mouse button, delete).

For the first and the last pot I act in the same way.

And There you go ! I was able to recover the two pots that interested me!

3. Cutout without mat!

The cutting tool has a third very interesting function: The preparation of our work for the extra large cut.

Here I take the sentence: create the life you want (Create the Life You Want # MC073C1A French Inspirational Phrases).

In parentheses, I recommend the cartouche linked to this expression which groups together all the sentences.

Create the life you want is one of my bikes! I find this sentence so inspiring! Our entire future is in our hands, and with our 10 fingers, we are solely responsible for creating our desires!

As you know you cannot cut more than 11.5 "x 11.5" "shapes. It's pretty boring but here's a tip if you want to cut it bigger. This involves squaring your image with 29.2cm squares that you cut out with the Cutout tool. Let's go!

I resume my sentence which I put to the desired size.

I reduce the canvas scale to see more clearly.

Now I add a 29.2cm square. I advise you to duplicate it a good amount of times so as not to have to put a square back to the right size each time

I place it so as to hide the upper left edge of my sentence

Beginner's mistake

During the installation of the grid the Design Space crashed. After all my image is very big and fat, which slows down the whole system...

And its solution

I advise you to save your project often during the grid because your pc may have more trouble reacting!

Once the square is well placed, select the square and the sentence you are cutting. You therefore have 4 pieces: the cut square, the cut out sentence, the cut out sentence a second time (remember the cookie cutter picture) and the rest of the sentence.

You can keep both elements of the sentence and delete the rest

We start again with a second square and so on until your sentence is squared

Be sure to always take the "piece" of the same color. Here it is not the case for me, so I will synchronize the colors via the synchronize button to the right of Layers on the layers panel.

Cricut Pens

Hello Crafter, if you are here, I can tell you that you are not the only person who has doubts about how to use Cricut pens in the correct way, because Cricut has several models that allow us to obtain multiple results, but to make them look good, you have to know how to configure them.

Therefore, in this section I will answer the following questions:

- What can I do with Cricut pens? o How to use Cricut pens?
- What styles are there in Cricut pens?
- How to set up Cricut pens the right way?

First, I explain everything you can create with these Cricut pens or markers.

If you work with projects for children, you will love this option, since with these markers you can create coloring pages for the little ones in the house.

Also, you can write your cards, part of your scrapbook layouts and even create labels for home organization from any of your cricut machines.

So, no matter which Cricut machine you have available, with all its models you can write or draw. The only thing you have to take into consideration is that cricut joy uses a different type of marker than its explore and maker sisters.

Now, I explain the variety of markers that cricut has available to work with.

- **Glitter gel 0.8** Ideal for formal invitations such as weddings, they will give a special touch to the name of the guests.
- **Marker 1.0** With a thicker effect you can highlight the part you prefer of the text.

- **Extra fine Point 0.3** These are ideal for writing longer texts.
- **Gel pen 1.0** They have a greater intensity in their strokes.
- **Fine Point** These are the most common pens in the cricut family and due to their thickness, they can be used in multiple ways. (and it's the style of scoreboard that cricut brings to all of their machines).

On the other hand, there are also a variety of markers that allow us to work on infusible ink projects, so we can draw with the machine or with our hands and then transfer them to the surface of our choice.

Infusible Ink Markets

Before we begin, let me explain that Infusible Ink is a new technique developed by Cricut which allows the ink to adhere to the material making it look like a print. This technique lasts much longer in the personalized article since its result is very similar to sublimation. Therefore, it is a good technique to include in your creative business or simply use it in your different crafts projects.

It is important to note that infusible ink is more delicate to handle than other forms of customization, however, with practice you will be able to master the technique quickly, you just have to remember a few additional steps compared to iron-on. Also, always apply heat in a straight line. So let's get started: To discuss the use of this new technique I will divide it into several chapters, as there are multiple options to consider. I'll start with the infusible ink markers. They come with different thickness at the tips which allow you to write in a fine way or fill / draw spaces with the others. Also, there are a variety of basic colors to play with.

Markers on T-shirts.

- The materials and tools for this project are:
- T-shirt compatible with infusible ink.
- Markers.
- Transfer paper.
- Protection paper.
- Heat resistant adhesive tape.
- Easy press 2.
- Mat easy press.

Important points for optimal use.

Use t-shirts with a perfect blend of polyester. As long as you have a high polyester surface you can do the test. In my case, I'm playing it safe and I'll be using the Cricut brand.

For these projects you must be extra careful with the materials you are working with and especially the cleaning in the area that you are going to customize since, if it is not totally clean, when the heat touches the material it expels the ink and can release particles that adhere as little blue dots all over the project. Since this is something we definitely don't want, we are going to wash our hands before we start and use a lint remover after applying heat to prepare the space to be personalized.

The temperature for these projects varies depending on the material you are going to work on. This time it will be: 385 f° at 40 seconds. But remember that you can always lean on the Cricut hub to verify that your temperature and time settings are correct . In addition, this help center can be used when you go to work with other Cricut brand materials.

When you work with t-shirts, you should always protect the material by inserting a piece of cardstock to prevent the ink from adhering to the other side of your t-shirt or the mat, since the infusible ink is activated by contact with heat and could again impregnate the ink from a previous project or damage current or future projects.

Important: Protect your markers even when they are not in use, store them in a space where they are not so hot. Preferably a cool and open space. Always with its lid on well, obviously!

EYE: this is essential! Make sure your design stays within the heat area of your Easy Press, as you can only heat press once .

I mean, you must ensure that your design is completely within the gray base of the easy press 2, since if we press twice to complete the transfer (as we can sometimes do with iron on) it could completely ruin the project.

Step by step of the Project with markers:

- Send the design to be drawn with the mirror function activated.
- Place the heat mat underneath and the cardstock inside the t-shirt.
- Preheat the t-shirt.
- Clean the t-shirt with the lint remover.
- Place the design in the space to personalize and add adhesive tape for heat, so it will not move.
- Place heat resistant paper for protection.
- Heat WITHOUT putting pressure on the area.
- Wait for it to cool down a bit and remove the paper.

Before concluding, I want to emphasize that you can also draw hands-free, whether you draw the silhouette with the Cricut and then want to add color with your hands or create your own design from scratch. What you should consider is that to transfer the art, it works the same as iron-on and if there is text it must be upside down so that when transferring it to the surface it is clear what you will capture there.

This is the final result of the first project with the Infusible Ink and the Easy Press 2. If you want to see another option of materials to personalize t-shirts.

So, I hope this helps you to start creating durable custom t-shirts with the new infusible ink technique that will be functional for your creative projects or businesses.

Quick Swap Tools

When Cricut launched the Maker, they made a promise to introduce more tools and materials so that we can grow alongside them as we master new craft techniques. Therefore, these tools provide more possibilities to create projects for

different creative businesses, mainly stationery.

So these new tools are proof that Cricut is taking the time to launch quality products and with the intention that we can create more and more beauty.

Before starting the project, I emphasize that these tools can only be used with Maker as it was specially designed for the adaptive tools system. This is a system that brings together three main technologies that provide versatility and professional cutting performance, therefore:

• Offers 10 times (4 kg) or more cutting force than the Explore line.

• Uses a sophisticated steering system to actively control the direction of the blade at all times.

• Tests to make sure you are using the correct blade before you start to cut and instructs us to replace it if it is not the correct one.

This time, and to test the Cricut tools, I will make a beach card with some vacation coupons. My husband and I will be married for two years and I have prepared a surprise trip for him! So, I will give you this card on which I will use the new toys for the Cricut Maker. Here is the creation process and the explanation of the different Cricut tools that I am using.

Punching Knife for Basic Tearing :

Perforation lines are evenly spaced to allow for a clean tear without the need for bending beforehand, this is ideal for handling bends of curvy shapes. It's also perfect for ripping pages out of brochures, raffle tickets, home magazines, or for any project that requires a good tear off.

I am using these lines to create some coupons, which we will use to carry out different activities during the holidays and will be pasted on the beach card.

Wavy cutting blade:

Add a wavy edge to any design with the specially sculpted stainless steel blade. It's great for original stickers, envelopes, cards, gift tags, or anytime you need fabulously finished edges with a sleek design.

For this project, I will place the wavy lines around the beach card. So I will give you a feeling of the sea.

Embossing point:

This embossing tool has a wider range of motion and gives you freedom to customize and design with incredible complexity. Add superior elegance to paper crafts by creating detailed raised designs.

You can create dimensional wedding cards, monogrammed thank you cards, gift box embellishments, tags, and more to create a striking effect.

Continuing with the card, I decided to use the tool to add more details to the sheets that will cover the text and coupons.

The other tools in the "quick swap" category are:

Engraving tip:

The Engraving Tip for Cricut Maker lets you add custom text or create monograms, draw embellishments and decorations, or engrave your favorite quotes on a variety of materials. For an eye-catching effect, etch onto Cricut aluminum sheets or anodized aluminum to reveal the silver color below.

Marking wheels (two options available):

Scoring Wheels for Cricut Maker create crisp marks on a variety of materials for effortless, perfect folds and a flawless finish.

In short, these new tools expand the possibility of creating unique and sophisticated projects. Likewise, we see Cricut's commitment to further expanding the capabilities of the Maker.

You probably already want to buy these tools for your creative business or simply to make your projects look good, and maybe at the moment you don't have much budget. My recommendation is that you can simply buy the adaptable pieces and with a single body or housing base you can use them all.

Tips to Store Bookmarkers

THERE IS NO DOUBT ABOUT THE LOVE WE HAVE FOR OUR MATERIALS! And it is very painful to see when one is damaged or does not work. Properly storing your materials helps improve their performance, their lifespan and obviously saves you money. In addition to that, not having them properly organized is difficult for you to find the color you want. Do you easily lose your bookmarks? Do you have markers that dry really fast? Do you always find dull colored pencils?

1. STORE YOUR DOUBLE-ENDED MARKERS HORIZONTALLY.

If you store these dual-tip markers upright, the ink will stay on one tip and the other will possibly dry out. Storing them flat will also make them last longer because the ink is less likely to dry out. Markers that should be stored in this way are, for example, Spectrum Noir, Winsor and Newton, and Copic Markers.

Note: The tom bows dual brush pens are not going into this category and can be stored vertically without any problems.

2. SINGLE-ENDED MARKERS

These markers depend on the consistency of their ink, the essential thing is that you store them with the tip down, but be careful with the pens type "gel" or better called " gel pens " that if you place them with the tip down it could spill very easily the ink making a mess; These can be stored with the tip up or horizontally.

3. COLORED PENCILS

The colored pencils since their pigment is not liquid you can store them in the way you want but taking the following notes:

If it is vertical, make sure the tips are facing up, they are less likely to break and you will not have to sharpen them every time you use it.

If it's horizontal, try placing a piece of fabric or foam over the tips to protect them.

4. GENERAL TIPS

You should keep your tools in a container when you are working to prevent them from falling to the ground and breaking or spilling more ink. If you use many at the same time in the same job, I recommend having a small tray, glass or cup on hand to hold them, so that you do not have to keep searching through your entire collection to use the same color over and over again, plus you avoid roll off your work surface. You can get divider trays for this and your drawers.

5. DON'T MELT YOUR COLORED PENCILS

Another tip is to keep colored pencils away from direct light or heat, as to our surprise the tip can achieve a "melted" effect that does not hold the pigment enough and makes the tip break easier.

6. APPRECIATE YOUR OWN RAINBOW

Organize your markers in groups of similar colors. To make this easier you can make sections like the rainbow or the basic color wheel, so it will be easier for you to find the color you want.

7. KEEP YOUR MARKERS AND PENCILS TIGHTLY CLOSED.

Some manufacturers claim they can last 24 hours without a cap and will continue to work well; It may work, but the ink may keep evaporating and becoming waste so better keep them covered all the time.

Easy Cricut Projects

Wall Decoration

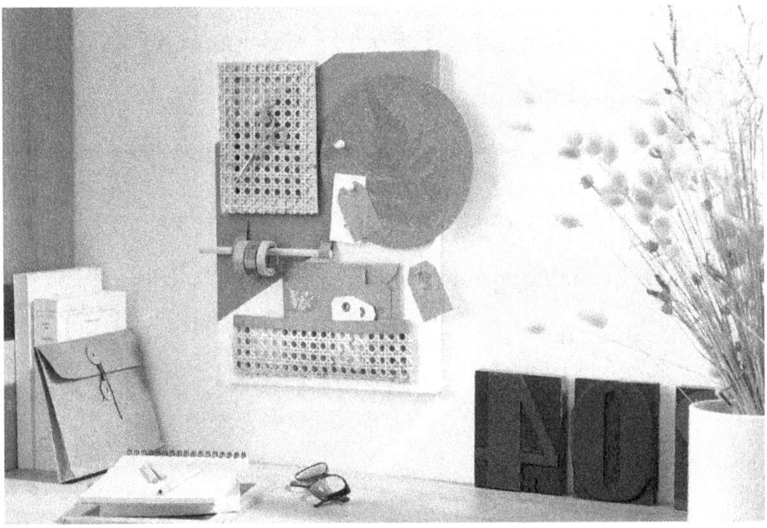

Use a magnetic board to make a wall decoration in natural colors and organize your office things as well as possible.

The necessary equipment:

- Magnetic canvas 30 x 40 cm and 6 extra strong magnets Ø 10 mm
- Natural cane 30 x 100 cm
- Round Cork plate 20 cm

- Pine frame 10x15 cm
- Acrylic multi-media - Matte White , matt fir green and gray mouse mat - 59 ml
- Wooden baguette
- Cricut Machine
- Imitation leather Kraft paper braiding tape - 9.5 cm
- Synthetic brushes flat n ° 16 and round n ° 4
- Paint roller
- Masking tape - 50m x 19mm - Monali
- A4 Cultura tracing paper
- B Monali graphite pencil
- Glue gun
- Templates to download

The stages of realization:

1. Prepare the paint mixture with 1/3 green, 1/3 white and 1/3 gray.
2. Draw two parallel diagonals on the canvas and stick masking tape on each side, then paint in between.
3. Download and print the fern template and trace it onto a sheet of tracing paper. All this using Cricut machine.

4. Place the tracing paper upside down on the cork support and iron with a grease pencil on the lines in order to transfer the pattern.
5. Paint the pattern.
6. Disassemble the frame to keep only the wooden outline.
7. Cut a piece of cane the size of the frame and glue it to the front of the frame.
8. Glue 4 magnets to the 4 corners of the back of the frame.
9. Download and print the pocket template and cut the caning to get the same shape.
10. Glue strips of kraft on the 4 sides of the back of the caning to solidify it.
11. Glue a strip at the top, on the front, for the finish.
12. To form the pocket, fold and fold the bottom of the cane inwards, then the two sides.
13. Glue the whole with a dot of glue, where the bottom and sides meet.
14. Cut two 12 cm kraft strips. Fold them in half and glue the ends. Slide the wooden stick through the formed loops.
15. Snap the frame onto the magnetic canvas. Then place the other elements in order to visualize their location, then glue them with the glue gun.

16. The magnetic canvas is ready to decorate your desk.

Customize you Snack Bag

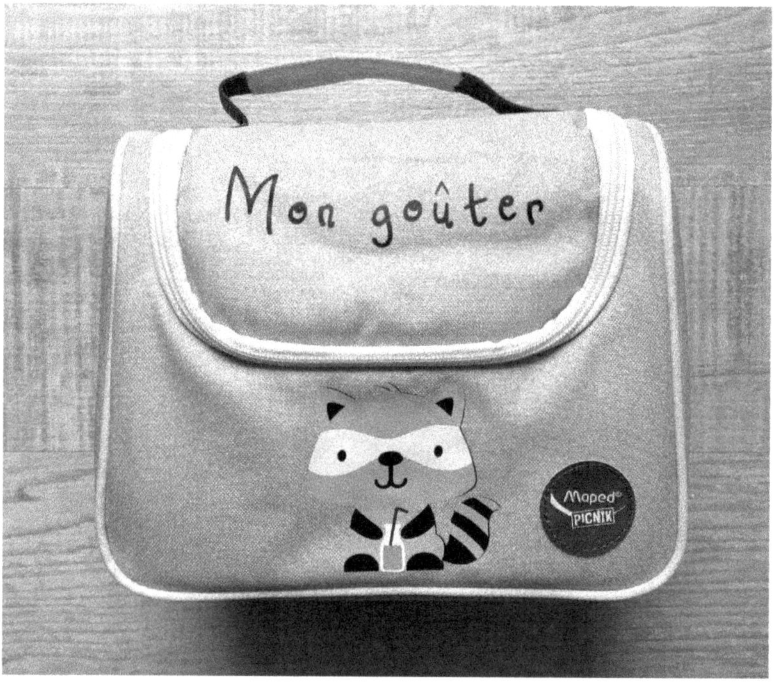

Now is the perfect time to personalize the snack bag (for your little ones and grown-ups!) With the Cricut cutting machine!

Here is the material you will need:

- a Cricut cutting machine (Cricut Maker , Cricut Explore Air2 or Cricut Joy)

- a snack bag - Maped

- iron- on adhesive in several colors. I chose black, white, gray, blue and red.

- Cricut EasyPress mini machine

- a cutting mat

- scissors (found in the Cricut precision tool set of 5)

- a stripping hook (found in the Cricut precision tool set of 5)

- a scraper

Procedure:

1. On Design Space, prepare your project.
2. Start the cut by clicking on CREATE and follow the instructions. Select the Everyday IRON-ON material. Don't forget to click on mirror. Place the iron-on patch on your cutting mat, shiny side against the mat. Put the mat in the notches of the machine and press the buttons as requested on your screen.
3. When the cut is complete, unload the mat. Now, it's time for weeding.
4. With the weed hook, remove the material you do not need.
5. Without forgetting the small pieces inside the drawing.

6. Repeat the operation on all the cuts.
7. Before taking the break with the EasyPress mini, you need to prepare your media. For this you need: an Easy Press Mini, a terry towel, baking paper.
8. Now place the terry towel in the snack bag. Add a piece of parchment paper inside between the bag and the napkin.
9. Place the first layer of your project on the bag.
10. Cover with baking paper to protect the bag and apply the press (set to medium heat).
11. Gently peel off the plastic film from the iron-on patch.
12. Repeat with all the other cuts. To apply the design to the top of the bag, lay it flat on the napkin with baking paper in between.
13. Apply the text to the top of the bag. There you have it, you have personalized your child's snack bag!

Creative Herbarium

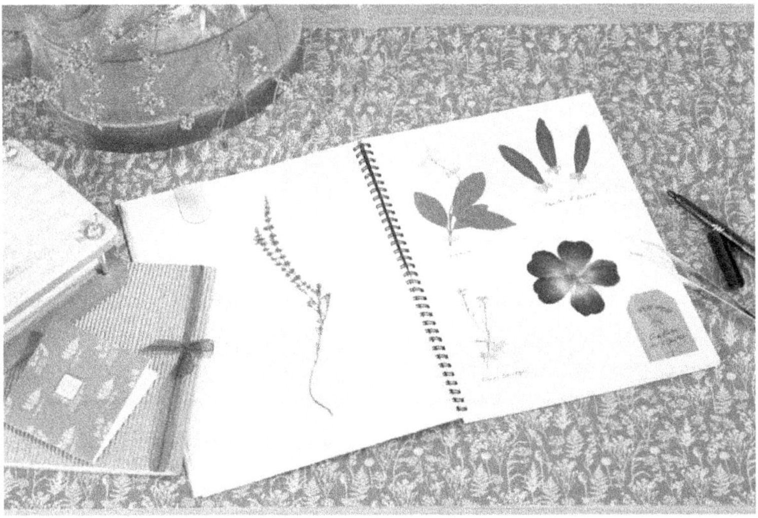

Learn how to dry your plants recovered in nature and collect them in your herbarium notebook or draw them in small drawing notebooks made yourself.

The necessary equipment:

- Scandicraft Collection Herbarium Album
- Block of 24 assorted printed papers A4
- Assortment of 3 sheets of stickers
- Wooden press "My herbarium"
- Drawing pad A5 80 sheets - 90g - Monali
- A4 paper cutter
- Cricut maker

- Assortment of 3 washi tapes
- Fine black felt pen
- Double-sided adhesive tape - 6mm x 10m
- Sewing needle
- Sewing thread
- 1 pair of scissors
- Downloadable envelope and notebook templates

The stages of realization:

1. Use of the press and the herbarium book 1. Collect fresh plants and flowers. Open the press to dry the plants. Take out the items: cardboard boxes, sheets of paper and foam.
2. Place a sheet of thin paper on cardboard. Position the plant to dry. Cut back the stem if necessary. Cover with a second sheet of thin paper. In addition to this, you need to know more about it.
3. Stack the cardboard boards on top of each other. Place in the press. Cover the last plant with a thin sheet and cardboard. Add the mousses. In addition to this, you need to know more about it.
4. Close the press on the plants. Screw as far as possible to crush the plants. Leave to dry for at least a week, especially for plants that are thick.

5. Gently remove the plants and flowers from the press. Open the herbarium notebook. Place the flowers and plants in the chosen location. Maintain with a piece of washi tape from the collection. Stick the rose with double-sided adhesive tape. Write the names of the plants. Stick a label to date the harvest and create a paper envelope to insert petals, seeds, etc.Creation of sketchbooks
6. Choose a paper from the collection. Fold in half crosswise. Measure 10.5 cm at the fold and cut with cricut. Take 4 sheets of drawing paper. Fold them in half and cut them in the same way as for the blanket.
7. Mark the points to be drilled at the fold of the sheets using the template to download in cricut. Pierce the leaves at the marks. Cut a sewing thread folded in 3. Pass the needle from the inside of the booklet to the cover. Bring the needle back to the center of the notebook and tie at the fold. Do the same for each pair of holes.
8. Cut the sheets that protrude from the notebook using the cutter. Decorate the cover with masking tape from the collection. Choose stickers and glue them in the center to finish decorating the cover. In addition to this, you need to know more about it.

9. Your notebooks are ready to be filled with pretty dried plants or drawn during your walks.

Fabric Pennant

The Cricut Maker machine gives you endless creative possibilities and one of the possibility is this fantastic project.

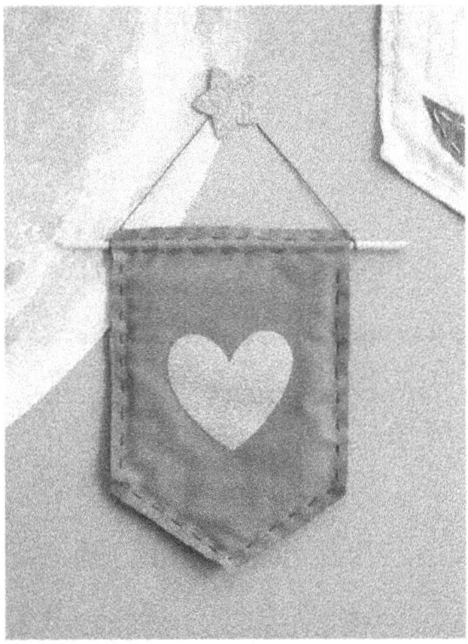

To make this tutorial, you will need:

- The Cricut machine

- Nice cotton fabric! - Discover our tissues on Cultura.com

- Tissue fusible golden - Discover the radius iron- on Cultura.com

- Fleece 100 x 100 cm Créalia - 150 g / m² - Créalia

- wooden rods

Discover all the steps below:

- For the first step, we start by cutting our fabrics with the Cricut machine to the desired shape. It is possible to use already existing templates or ideas via the CRICUT platform. For this DIY I decided to create my own shape for my banner. We therefore take care of cutting our formats to then mount our pennant and also cut the elements with the iron-on paper. For the banner, you must therefore create 2 patterns of the same format that will then be associated!
- I decide to transfer my iron-on fabric to one side of my pennant. The great thing about this iron-on fabric is that we don't have to think about printing the design inside out. We only need an iron, a stable surface, a cloth or a very thin cloth to stick the element.
- We start to assemble our pennant, we take our two pieces of fabric that we will come to associate. We start by sewing the top of the banner, then directly place the wooden rod which will serve as a support for hanging!

- I wanted to give my pennant a little more volume, so I decided to integrate a fleece inside, which we cut to the approximate shape of our pennant. I cut here the fleece of a size relatively smaller than my fabric to have this filling effect and then in step 5 to be able to have enough room to come and sew all around! I allow myself to put 3 small dots of glue to fix my fleece and be sure that it will not move afterwards!
- We finish sewing all around our fabric to finally finish our pennant, everything is well hung. We can now add our little string and hang our pretty banner wherever you want!

Paperbox

This little word is very simple but it nevertheless has so much power ... Hidden in a box, you will be able to create a surprise and offer a THANK YOU full of love and tenderness to one of your loved ones or during a particular event.

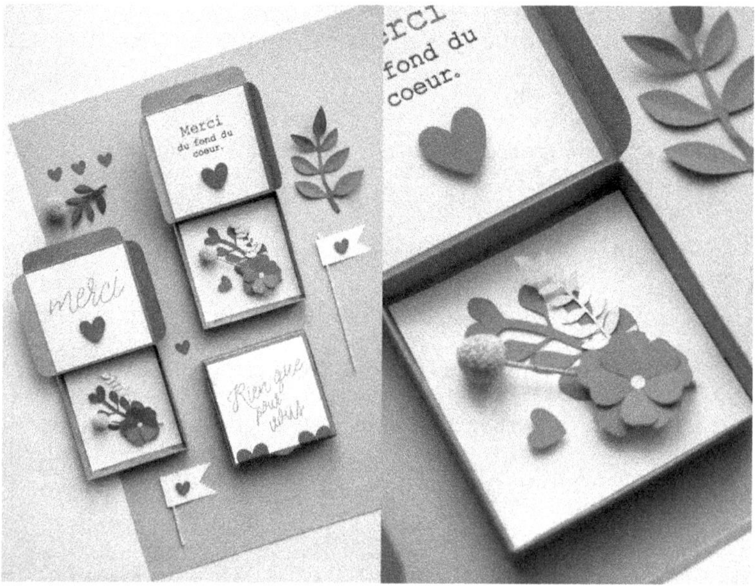

For this you will need:

- The Cricut Joy Machine
- Color papers
- Glue
- Removable gold vinyl

- Gold Marker - Cricut Joy
- The template that you will find attached
- The typos used are Courier new and Adelaide (the latter is from Cricut)
- For those who can log into Cricut, here is the Design Space project link.

Discover all the steps below:

1. Using your application prepare the cutting of your paper templates for your box, as well as the paper decorations (ex: foliage / flowers / hearts).
2. Using your application prepare the cutting of your paper templates for your box, as well as the paper decorations (eg: leaves / flowers / hearts).
3. Prepare to cut your heart stickers with your SMART VINYL REMOVABLE Gold paper which you will use to close your box.
4. Now that the paper templates are cut out, use your GOLD marker to create and draw your texts. You can choose to write whatever you want.
5. It's time to stick your papers on your cardboard box. The "Thank you" paper is to be placed inside the box on the upper part. Also place your plain pink paper template at the bottom of your box.

6. Now stick your paper with your text "Just for you" on the outside of the box.
7. Come and create your floral arrangement inside your box using strong glue, I decided to add a real craspedia to it so that I don't just have paper. Alternatively, you can add a branch of eucalyptus, or olive tree.
8. Once your interior decoration is finished, you can now close your box and seal it with your golden heart stickers. All you have to do is offer them.

T-shirt Printing

Although its cutting area is limited, you can combine vinyls in different sizes and with different textures to create a larger set like in this shirt that you can easily print it.

We explain how to do it:

- Upload your image, trace it and insert it into your workspace.
- Scale to the size you want to cut it.
- Now duplicate the layer and hit 'outline' at the bottom right.
- Click on hide all contours and select the parts you want to cut separately.
- Close and repeat the operation for the rest of the design.
- Now go to the sync tab, top right. Select a color for each part of the design that you are going to cut with a different vinyl.
- Hit do it. Choose 'on mat' and you will see that the designs have been automatically organized by color.
- Choose the material, as it is a turbo vinyl, we will choose everyday iron on.
- Remember to activate the mirror mode for textile vinyls.
- Put the vinyl on the mat, and load it. Click on go.

- When the cut is finished, it unloads the material.
- Now in the next cut we are going to change the material to cut the glitter vinyl, we will choose holographic sparkle Iron-On
- We load the vinyl on the mat and insert it into the joy.
- Repeat the operation for the rest of the colors.
- Carry out the removal of the vinyl with the help of peeling tools.
- Heat the iron to 160°C and program 5 seconds.
- Put the protective pad on the table.
- Place the shirt on top and pre-iron it for a few seconds
- Come up with the design and leave the first vinyl to iron on.
- Iron for 5 seconds with pressure.
- Remove the hot conveyor. If it gets up, hold on for a few more seconds.
- Repeat the operation for the rest of the vinyls.
- Perform a final 20 second ironing using protective paper and applying even pressure.

You can see how it turned out great!

Paper based Cricut Projects

Fruity Tray

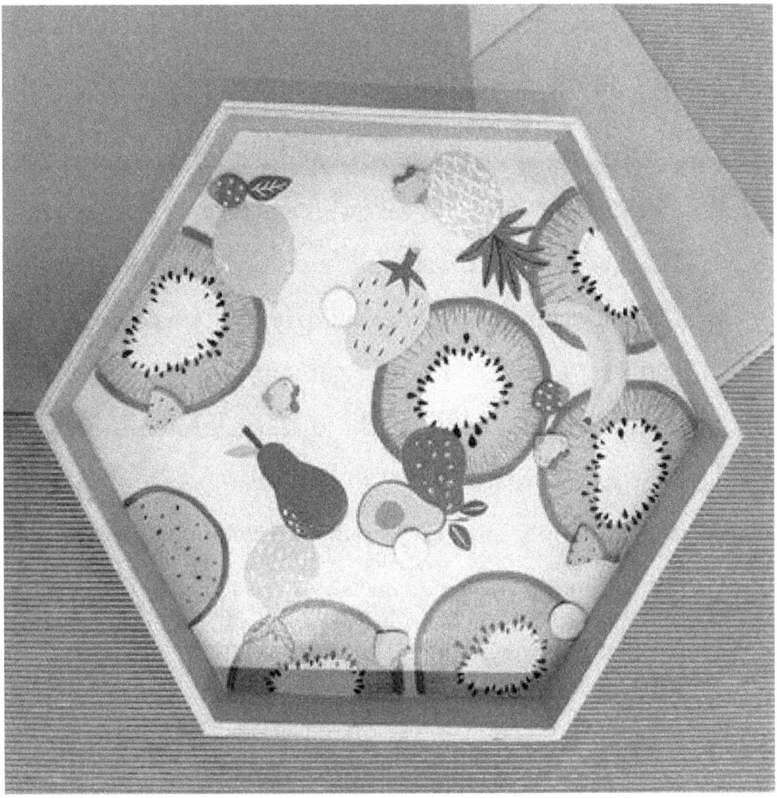

For this you will need:

- An octagonal tray, crealia coral, light yellow, white and leaf green decorative paints.

- One or two flat brushes
- A pencil
- A 10cm paper disc and brown
- Black and glitter green poscas
- Polish glue to varnish spray and masking tape.

Discover all the steps below:

1. Draw disks on your board and paint them green (mix leaf green with light yellow) it will be necessary to make 2 layers. After drying, make yellow ovals in the center (light yellow and white) and paint in two coats too. All this can be done using cricut template
2. Trace the outlines of the discs in brown. Draw the green lines (see photo) in the green area and then the pips. Apply a spray varnish to prevent the posca from drooling in the glue varnish in the next step.
3. Stick the stickers with the varnish glue in the bottom of the tray. After drying, apply a little varnish in spray to prevent the ink of the stickers from dissolving in contact with the resin.
4. Using a glue gun, attach the small wooden fruit decorations.

Here are some indications for a successful resin.

- First of all, the bottom of the tray must be varnished to prevent inks / colors / paints from bleeding into the paint. It is not systematic, but it could happen, so you better take the lead.

- Then, respect the dosages of the packaging and check that you pour the hardener first. - Mix for a long time. 10 minutes minimum per cup. Here there are two cups, I have mixed over 20 minutes. Don't hesitate to transfer your mixture to a new cup and mix again. - pour the resin in the center of the tray and distribute the whole by tilting it.

- let dry two days, even if the packaging says 24h.

Craft paper pencil holder

Discover the braiding of strips of kraft paper and make a pencil holder in natural colors for your office.

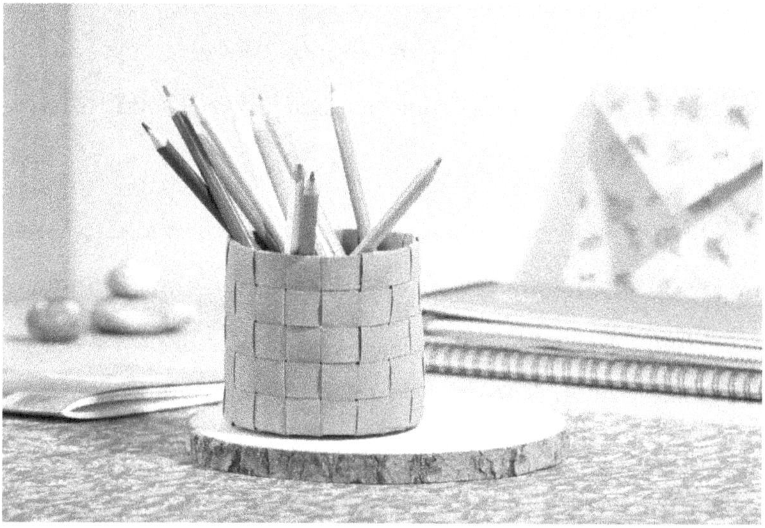

The necessary equipment:

- Imitation leather kraft paper braiding tape - 9.5 cm
- Self-healing cutting mat - 60x45 cm
- Transparent ruler for creative hobbies 40 cm
- Scissors
- Mini high temperature glue gun
- Pencil
- Salvaged cardboard, glass and jar or compass

Discover all steps below:

1. Take a glass and a jar with different diameters. Trace the outlines of the circles on recycled cardboard. Cut with a cutter. In addition to this, you need to know more about it.
2. Glue the cardboard discs together with the glue gun. Cut strips of kraft paper braiding 20 cm long. Glue them one by one in radiation. Superimpose them slightly at the base: the bands must be edge to edge at the circumference of the cardboard disc. In addition to this, you need to know more about it.
3. Cover the larger cardboard disc in this way. Glue with a glue gun. Fold the braiding strips, then measure the circumference of the cardboard disc and cut 5 braiding strips of this size. In addition to this, you need to know more about it.
4. Slide a strip of braiding perpendicular under one of those welded to the cardboard base. Stick one end to it, as close as possible to the base. Pass it alternately under one vertical strip and over the next one. Attach a dot of glue to the glue gun under a few vertical strips.
5. To close, glue the second end of the strip under the first end. In the same way, slip a second strip of

braiding, mount a second row, tightening to avoid gaping spaces.

6. Set up the braiding of the pot with 5 strips in all. Fold a base strip towards the inside of the pot. Mark the fold in the pot to mark the length. Cut off the excess. In addition to this, you need to know more about it.
7. Cut a strip of braiding a little larger than the circumference of the pot. Glue to the top edge of the pot with a glue gun. Fold the strips one by one towards the inside of the pot. Glue them with a glue gun. R with a glue gun.9. The pot is ready to accommodate the pencils in your office.

Birth announcement card

Make an announcement using different Parisian ties to celebrate the birth of your child.

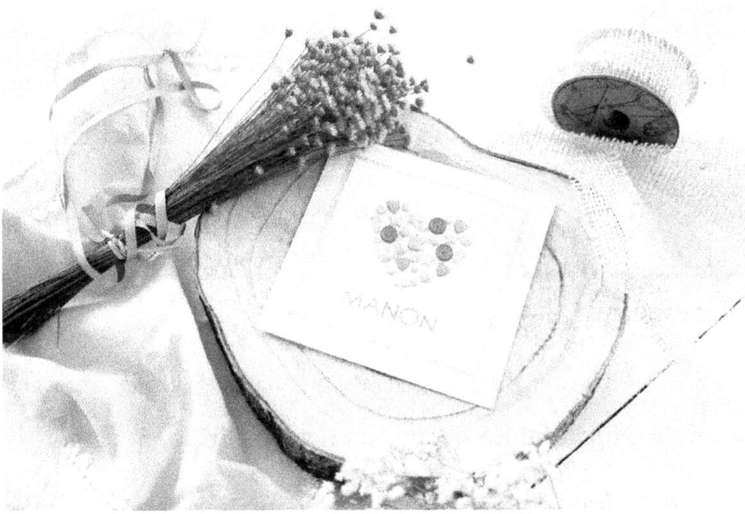

To make this invitation, you will need:

- Assortment of Parisian ties "newborn girl"
- Assortment of 80 Parisian ties - Pink
- Alphabet Glitter uppercase - Pink
- 25 Pollen folded cards 135x135 mm - White
- Mahé sheet 30.5 x 30.5 cm white
- Mahé sheet 30.5 x 30.5 cm pale pink
- Tube of universal gel glue - Cultura - 30 ml
- Precision cutter and 3 blades
- Self-healing cutting mat - 30x22 cm
- Assortment of 3 precision tools

- Transparent ruler for creative hobbies 30 cm
- Template to download and print

Discover all the steps below:

STEP 1/8 To start, download, print and reproduce the heart template. Hollow out the pattern using the cutter to create a stencil.

STEP 2/8 Cut an 11 x 11 cm pink square and a 10.5 x 10.5 cm white square.

STEP 3/8 Center the stencil on the square of white paper and secure it with adhesive paper, to prevent it from moving.

STEP 4/8 Place a few Parisian ties to guide you in their positioning, inside the cutout heart.

STEP 5/8 Using a precision cutter or paper punch, pierce your card and insert the Parisian clips.

STEP 6/8 Once the heart is filled, glue the white part on the rose.

STEP 7/8 Finish by pasting the desired text (first name ..) to finalize the card.

STEP 8/8 The invitation is ready.

Cloud Shelf

Decorate this shelf cloud beautiful papers to Koala reasons for decorating children's room very soft.

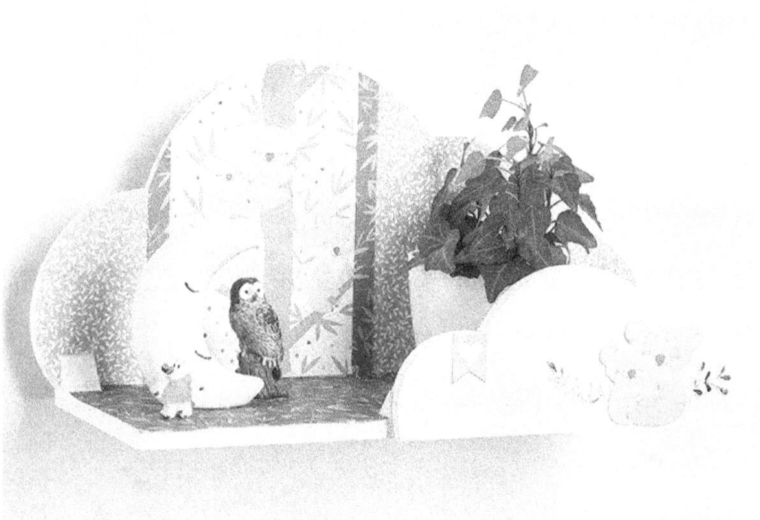

To make this cloud shelf, you will need:

- Créalia "Clouds" wooden shelf
- Acrylic tube 120 matt white
  3u7m,,,,,,,,,,,,,,,,bkjFlat synthetic brush n ° 18
- Straight scissors - 17 cm
- Transparent ruler for creative hobbies 30 cm
- Precision cutter and 3 blades
- Self-healing cutting mat - 45x35 cm

- Cardboard stickers - Little baby
- Extra strong double-sided adhesive tape - 6mm x 10m

Discover all the steps below:

STEP 1/6 Paint the cloud shelf white. Let dry.

STEP 2/6 Download and transfer the templates to different papers from the collection and compose the decoration.

STEP 3/6 Glue the cut papers on the cloud shelf using the extra strong double-sided tape.

STEP 4/6 Personalize the shelf with stickers from the collection.

STEP 5/6 Tip: the 30 x 30 cm block of paper offers visuals to frame to decorate your child's room or make scrapbooking albums.

STEP 6/6 The cloud shelf is ready to decorate your child's room

DIY Bookmark Cat-page

Here is the cat-page bookmark, your summer companion!

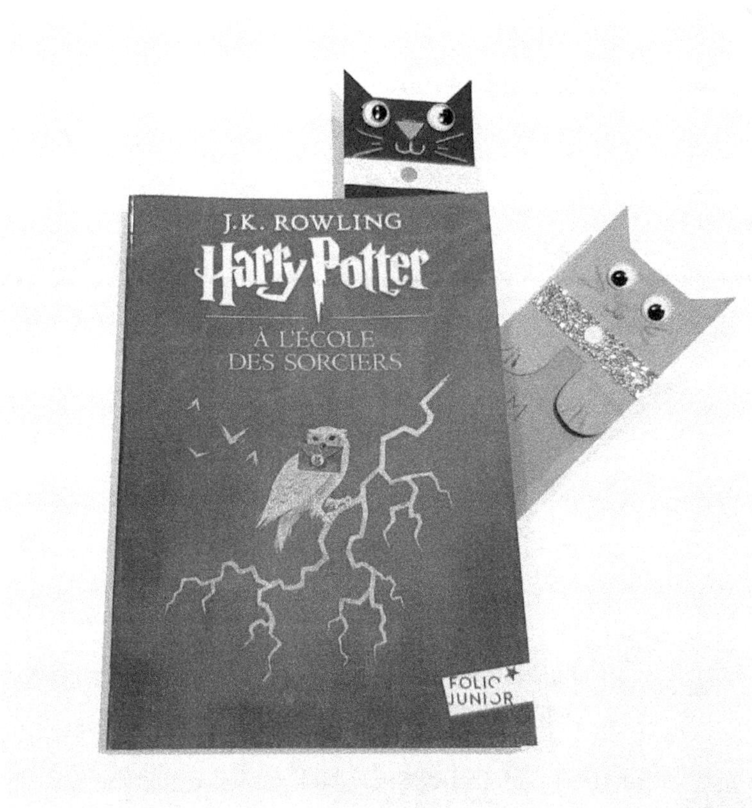

Materials used:

- -block of 20 multi-colored cartoline sheets
- Glue
- Pouch of 24 decorated colored pencils
- 6 round movable eyes Ø 12mm

- PERFO ROUND CLAMP 6MM
- 5m roll of Glitter masking tape - Green
- 5m roll of Glitter masking tape - White

Discover all the steps below:

1. Print the template and choose its paper colors.
2. Cut out the template along the lines.
3. Copy the drawing of the body, front legs and back legs on the brown sheet, do the same in the purple sheet for the belly and cut out.
4. Glue the elements together with glue.

** To facilitate the gluing put a little glue in a cardboard plate and use a brush to spread the glue well. Then clean the brush with warm water and soap.

5. Glue the movable eyes, glue a piece of masking tape to make the collar, cut a piece of pink paper in a triangle for the nose and with a black pencil draw the mouth, mustaches and legs.
6. With the hole punch, make a small circle in the yellow paper and glue it to finalize the cat's collar.

** To get an easy triangle nose, first cut out a square and cut it in half diagonally.

7. Write your name on the cat's belly with a colored pencil.
8. And there you have a nice cat-page bookmark for your summer readings. I'm going to rercad the adventures of the little wizard and what will you read?

You can even do it in other colors so that it doesn't get bored!

Table Decoration

Create a fresh and summery decoration for a tropical atmosphere, both on your walls and on your tables! Ideal for your summer evenings, to share without moderation!

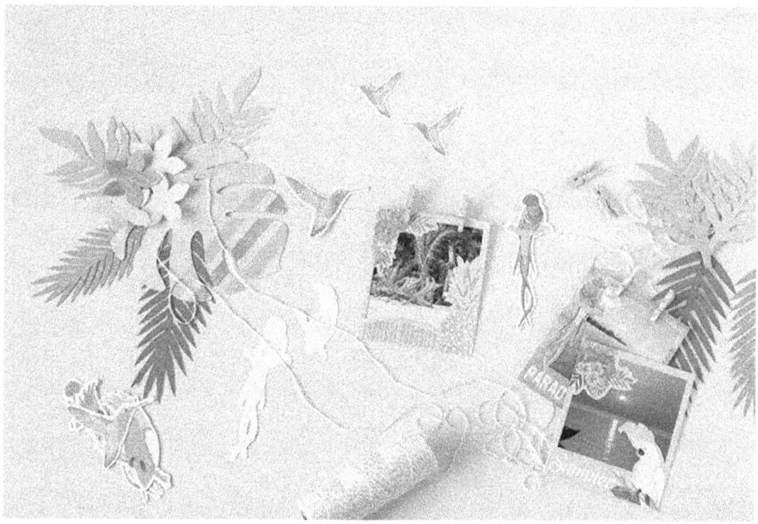

To make this tropical decoration, you will need:

- Set of 6 Scrapbooking paper sheets - Tropical Paradise
- Mahé Leaf - 30.5x30.5cm - petrol blue .
- Mahé Leaf - 30.5x30.5cm - menthol green
- Mahé Leaf - 30.5x30.5cm - lime green
- Mahé Leaf - 30.5x30.5cm - spring green

- Slate scrapbooking sheet - Mahé - 30x30cm
- Sheet of 34 epoxy stickers - Tropical Paradise
- 8 card stock polaroid frames - Tropical Paradise
- Assortment of 40 die-cuts - Tropical Paradise
- 100m two-tone spool - Sky blue
- 16 mini clothespins 35 mm
- Vivaldi smooth sheet A4 240g - Canson - white n ° 1
- Precision cutter and 3 blades
- Blue cutting mat - 2mm - A3
- Black acrylic and aluminum ruler 30cm
- Precision scissors 13.5cm blue bi-material rings
- 3D adhesive squares
- Mahé Tools - Easy Mounter - scrapbooking
- Pack of 6 HB graphite pencils

Find out below all the steps to make your "Tropical Paradise" summer decoration:

1. Gather the materials.
2. Using the template and a pencil, reproduce the palm tree on the papers in the collection.

1. Download and print the template here .
2. Cut out with a cutter or scissors.

3. Assemble the trunk of the palm tree. Glue the foliage. Using the template, reproduce the traces of the cocktail support on thin cardboard, following the dimensions indicated. Cover it with the collection paper.
4. Download and print the template here.

5. After having cut in the slate sheet: 1 x (8.5 x 8.5 cm). Choose a Polaroid. Glue the slate sheet to the back of the Polaroid. Using a chalk pen, write "Cocktail of the day". Decorate with the stickers. Fold the support at the dotted lines.
6. Using the templates and a pencil, draw the leaves and flowers on the Mahé paper and on the collection paper. Draw.
7. Download and print the leaf and flower template .
8. Choose photos. Cut them to size: 8.5 x 8.5 cm. Stick to the back of the Polaroids.
9. Glue the leaves and flowers together. Cut the string to the desired dimensions and glue it to the back of the flowers. Glue the birds on the string and hang the photos using mini clips.

And here is a pretty summer and tropical decoration! Beautiful evenings in perspective!

Clothespin Card

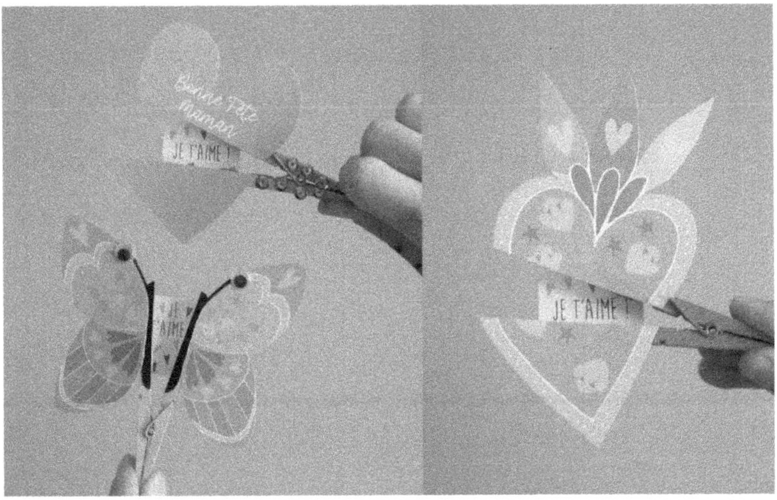

The necessary equipment:

- Clothespin
- Glue
- Painting
- Color paper or illustrations to download
- Decorations: eyes , sequins

The stages of realization:

1. Start by painting your clothespins.
2. Cut out the illustrations or your colored paper in a heart shape.
3. Come and cut your shape in half in the middle.
4. Apply glue to the ends of your clothespin.

5. And stick your heart or your butterfly on your clothespin.
6. We now add glue to the back of your clothespin to be able to place the small text "I love you".
7. You can also add small decorations to further customize your clothespin. Your laundry card is ready!

Easter Special Containment

It's time to collect at home..... Rolls of toilet paper, colored sheets, markers and glue

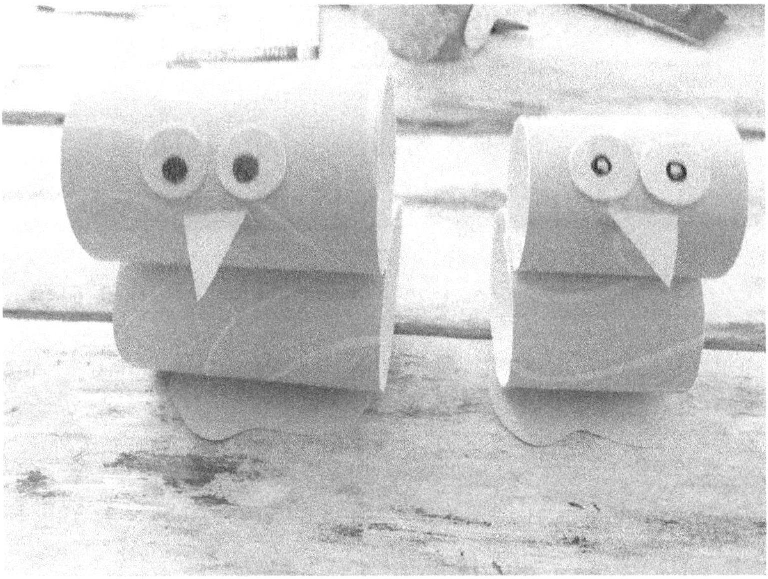

1. Cut the height measurements from your roll and glue by wrapping this paper around. With white glue or whatever you have at home.
2. Hold the paper with pins so that it sticks.
3. Then make a template to make ears that we transfer to a paper and that we cut.
4. With another paper, cut out the inside of the ears and glue them.

5. Now, we have to make the eyes.... either you have moving eyes or you do them yourself like me.... For that we make circles by hand or with perforators.
6. Glue the eyes and ears.
7. Make bunny papattes, cut them and glue them.
8. Draw the nose and whiskers with a felt tip pen.
9. Now we're going to make the paper chick ...
10. Cut 2 rectangles in paper here 6x14 and 6x12
11. Staple the papers together to make rolls. And superimpose them as below.
12. Cut out beaks and eyes, then glue them.
13. Cut out some feet, glue them and your chicks are ready!!!

Boat Garland

Here is a garland on the Marine theme to navigate according to our creativity.

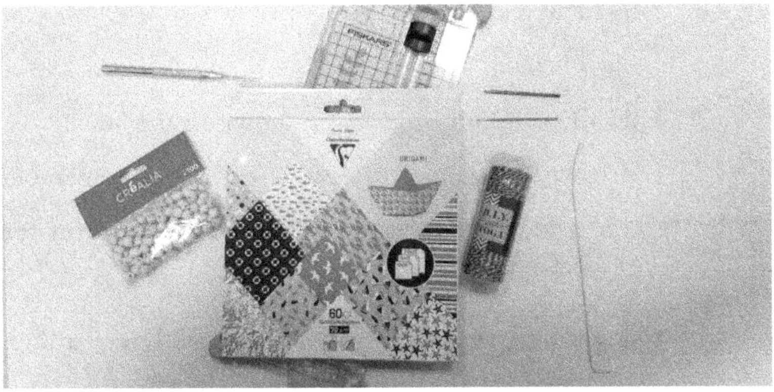

Equipment:

- Marine origami papers 70 g / m², Clairefontaine

- 8mm wooden beads, Créalia

- Two-tone blue and white twine, Toga

- A folder

- A paper piercer

- A needle with a large eye

- A cutter

- A pair of scissors

1. Cut the origami papers of different sizes, you need:

- of 7cm x 10cm
- 3 of 10.5cm x 15cm
- 3 of 14cm x 20cm

2. Fold the different squares as shown in the small boat construction diagram below. At each step, remember to use a folder to facilitate folding and not to tear the paper
3. Using the paper punch, pierce the small boats at their tops.
4. Cut 1m of two-colored string. Make a loop 50cm from the wire so that it is in the middle.
5. Using the needle, thread alternately a bead and then a small boat (from the smallest to the largest). Each element must be blocked with a small double knot. Finish with a double knot below the last boat and cut the excess thread that protrudes.
6. All you have to do is hang your garland!

Cricut Projects with Illustrated Steps

Wedding Table Plan

Completion time: more than 2 hours.

Difficulty: 1/3

To make your plant wedding table plan, you will need:

- Cricut Machine

- 1 box of 25 Pollen sheets 210x297 mm 210g - Ivory

- Extra strong double-sided adhesive tape - 6mm x 10m -

- High temperature glue gun -

- White metal ring 25 cm -

- Straight scissors 17 cm -

- 1 natural kraft string -

Discover all the steps below:

STEP 1/13 Using the cricut, cut multiple sheets using the different shades of green card stock.

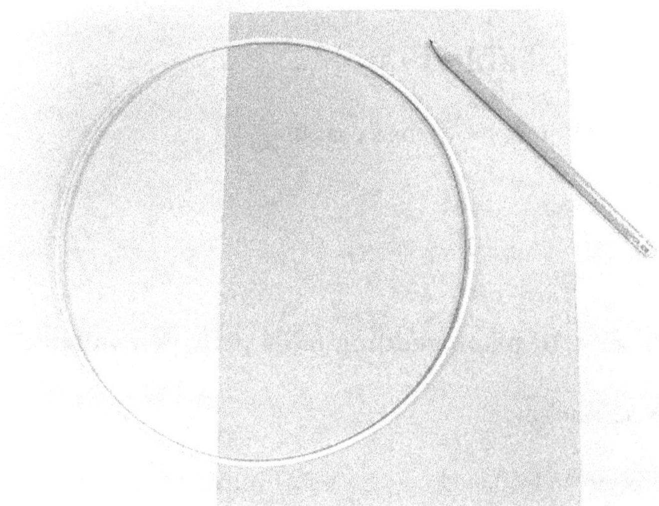

STEP 2/13 Trace the inner and outer outline of the half of the ring on green card stock with a pencil, and cut out the half moon, leaving enough room on both sides to be able to fold it around the ring.

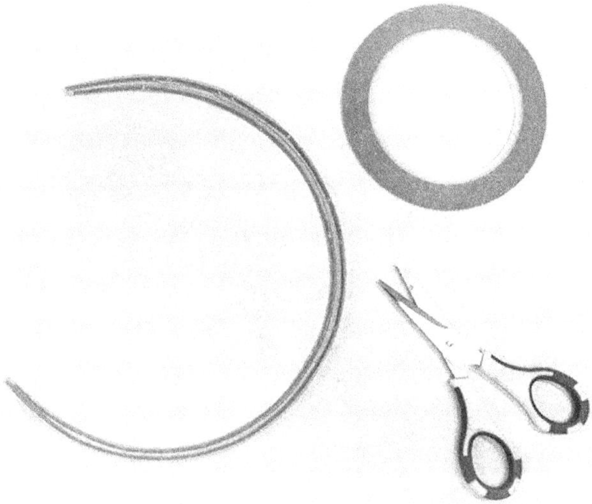

STEP 3/13 Stick the double-sided adhesive tape on the half-moon.

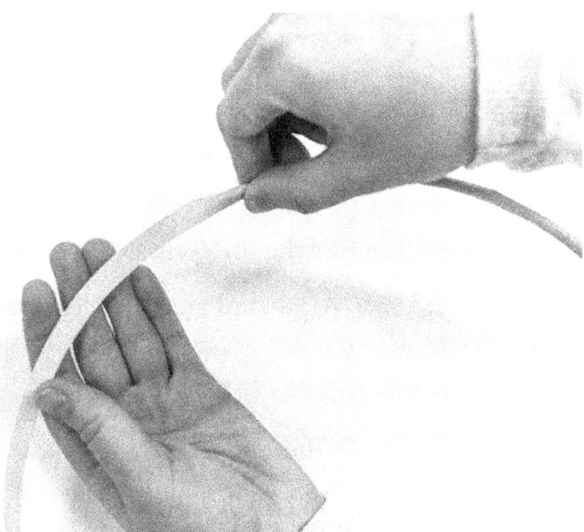

STEP 4/13 Fold it around half of the hoop, pinching the edges so that they are secure. This edge will serve as a base for easily gluing your paper sheets.

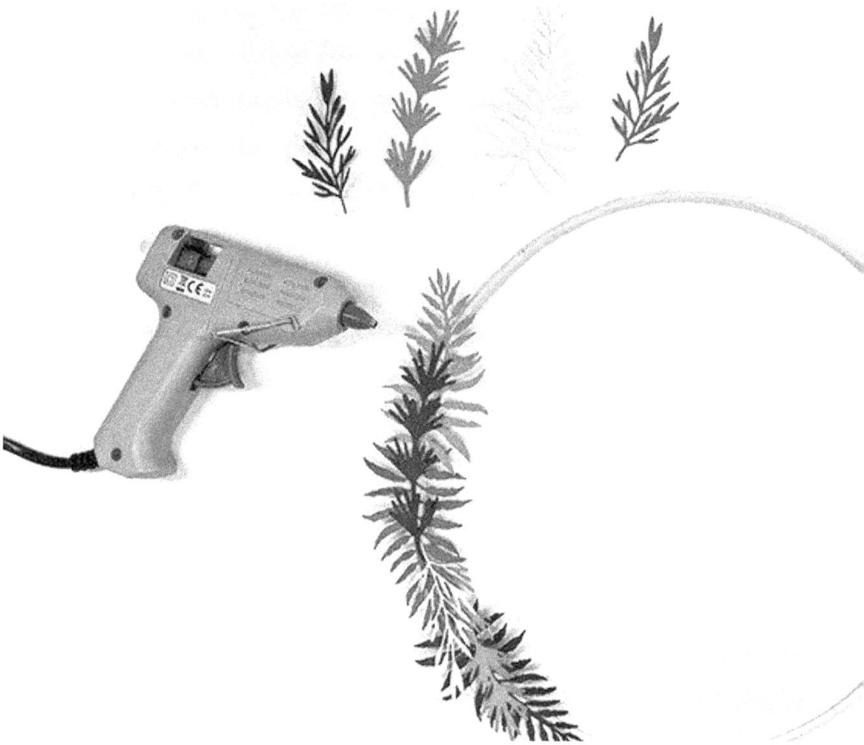

STEP 5/13 Arrange the different cut sheets on the part of the ring covered with paper and glue the elements with a glue gun.

STEP 6/13 Using the cricut and the Natural Leaves die, cut the berries out of the cream card stock.

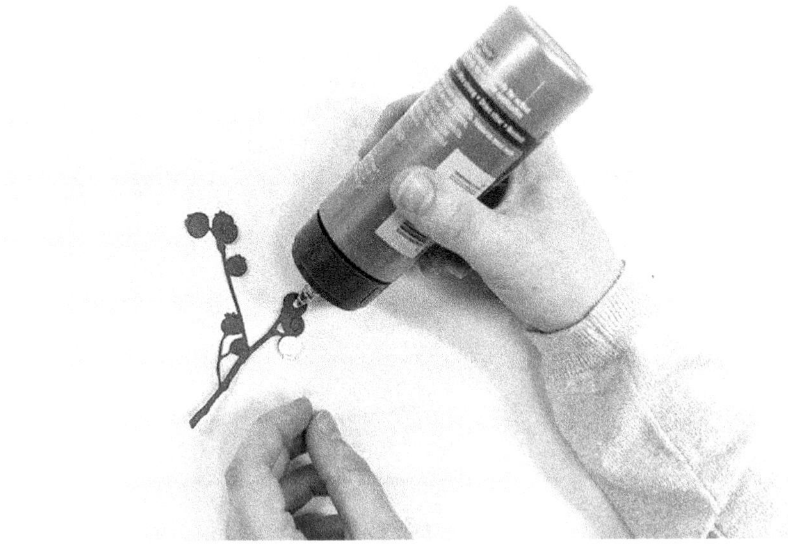

STEP 7/13 Glue the berries on the corresponding branches of the set to bring out the berries.

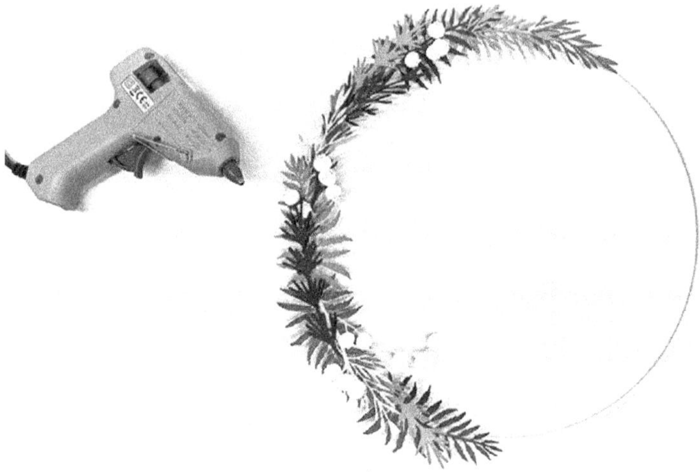

STEP 8/13 Insert and glue the berry branches among the other leaves where you want to add shades of color.

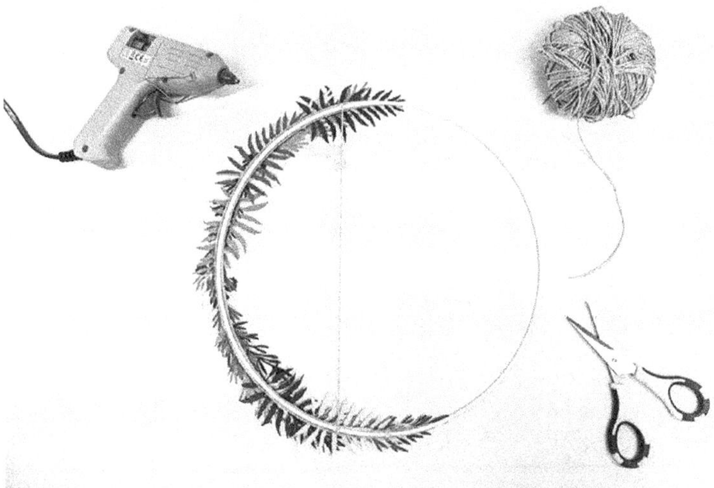

STEP 9/13 Tie the string to the back of the metal ring with the glue gun, cut off the excess if necessary

STEP 10/13 Print the table numbers on the cream card stock, cut out in a circle and glue it on the string, towards the center of the ring.

STEP 11/13 Print the names of the guests on the cream paper and cut them out with scissors, forming banners.

STEP 12/13 Create your seating plan and paste the guest names wherever you want!

STEP 13/13 Create as many rings as there are guest tables for your wedding and arrange them on a recovered wooden pallet.

Paper Decoration

To make this tropical decoration, you will need:

- Cricut

- Set of 6 Scrapbooking paper sheets -

- Leaf - 30.5x30.5cm - petrol blue .

- Leaf - 30.5x30.5cm - menthol green

- Leaf - 30.5x30.5cm - lime green

- Leaf - 30.5x30.5cm - spring green

- Slate scrapbooking sheet - 30x30cm

- Sheet of 34 epoxy stickers -

- 8 card stock polaroid frames -

- Assortment of 40 die-cuts -

- 100m two-tone spool - Sky blue

- 16 mini clothespins 35 mm

- Vivaldi smooth sheet A4 240g - Canson - white n ° 1

- Precision cutter and 3 blades

- Blue cutting mat - 2mm - A3

- Acrylic and aluminum ruler 30cm black

- Precision scissors 13.5cm blue bi-material rings

- 3D adhesive squares

- Mahé Tools - - scrapbooking

- Pack of 6 HB graphite pencils

Preparation time: 2h

Techniques: Stencil, Collage, Origami - Folding, Tropical

Discover below all the steps to realize your summer decoration "Tropical Paradise":

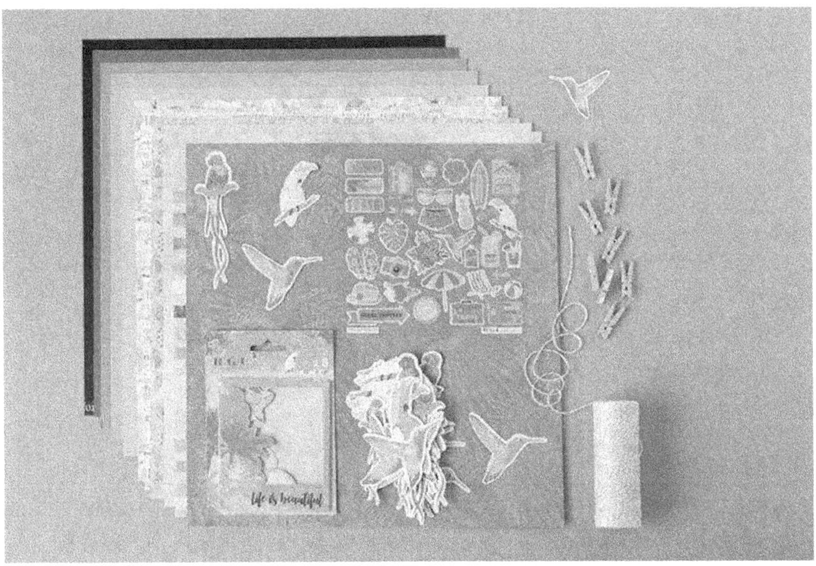

1. Gather the materials.

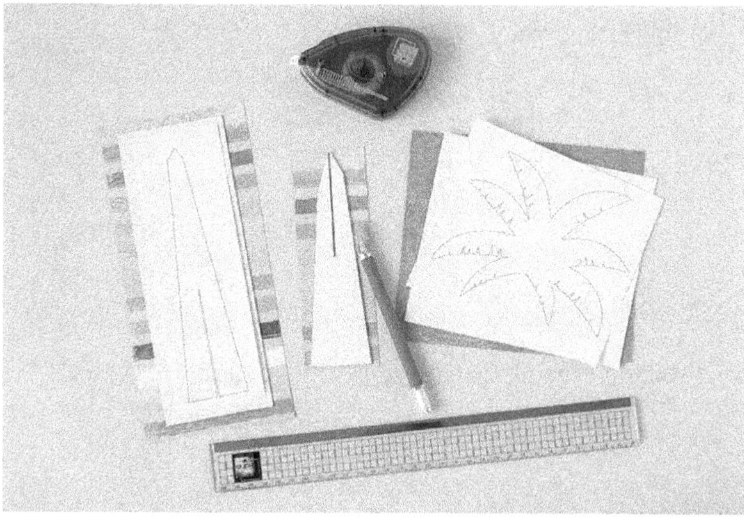

2. Using the template and a pencil, reproduce the palm tree on the papers in the collection.

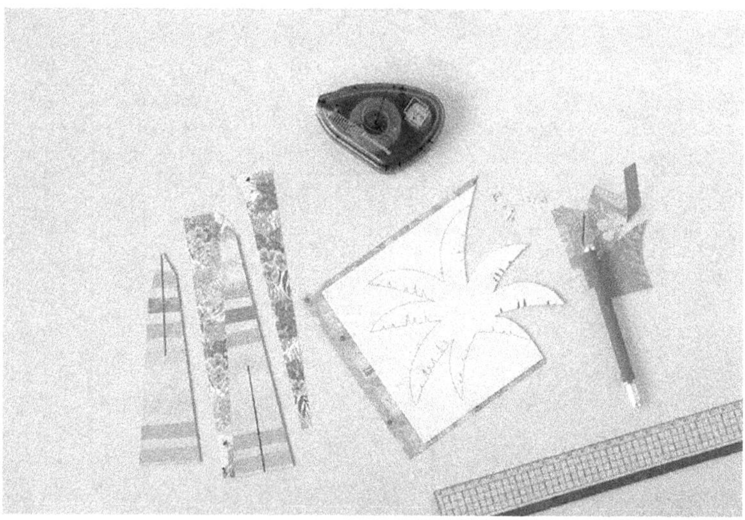

3. Cut out using cricut.

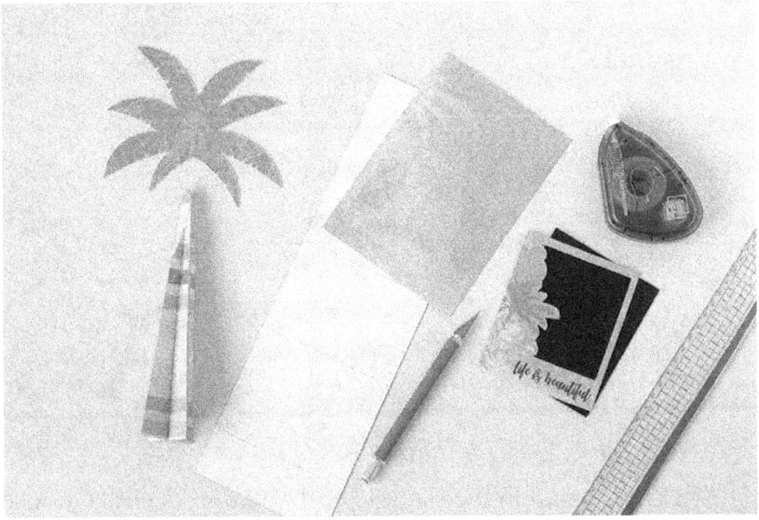

4. Assemble the trunk of the palm tree. Glue the foliage. Using the template, reproduce the traces of the cocktail support on thin cardboard, following the dimensions indicated. Cover it with the collection paper.

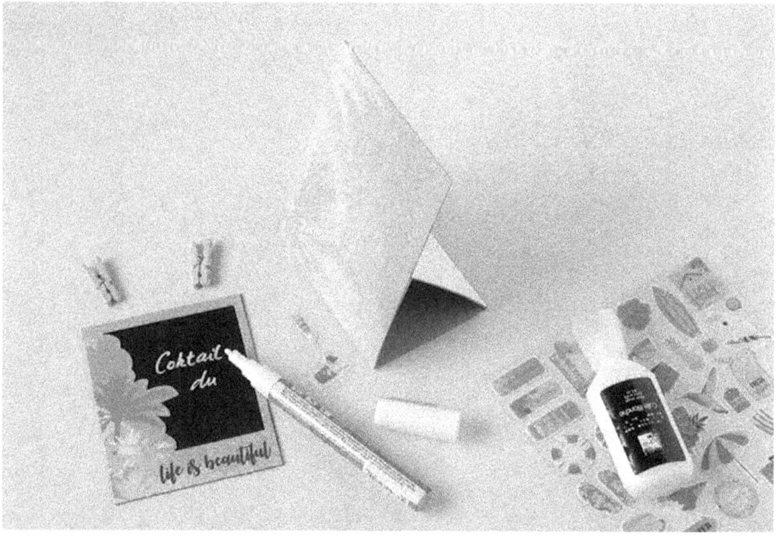

5. After having cut in the slate sheet: 1 x (8.5 x 8.5 cm). Choose a Polaroid. Glue the slate sheet to the back of the Polaroid. Using a chalk pen, write "Cocktail of the day". Decorate with the stickers. Fold the support at the dotted lines.

6. Using the templates and a pencil, draw the leaves and flowers on the paper and on the collection paper. Draw.

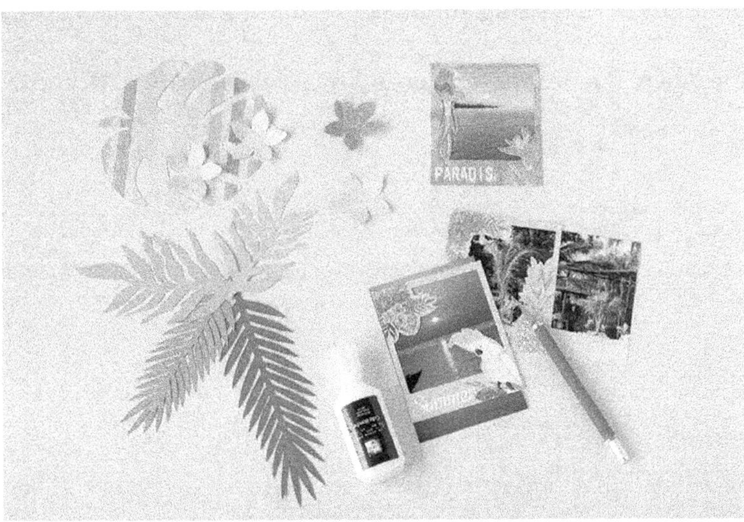

7. Choose photos. Cut them to size: 8.5 x 8.5 cm. Stick to the back of the Polaroids.

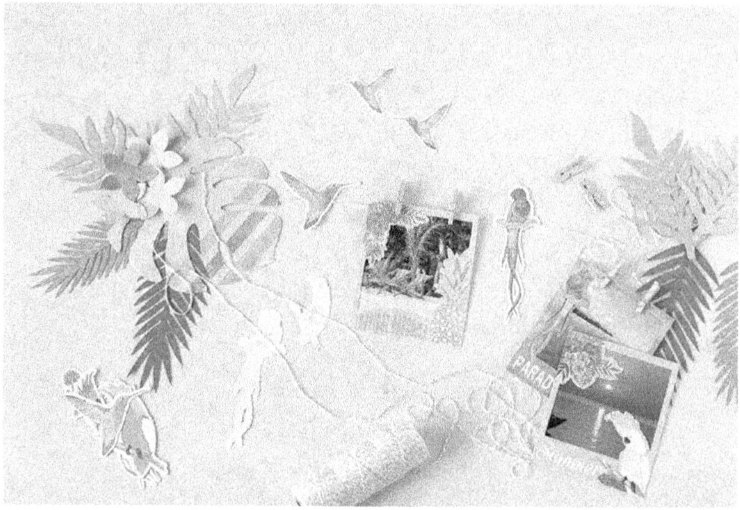

8. Glue the leaves and flowers together. Cut the string to the desired dimensions and glue it to the back of the flowers. Glue the birds on the string and hang the photos using mini clips.

And here is a pretty summer and tropical decoration! Beautiful evenings in perspective!

Crepe Paper Flowers

Completion time: more than 2 hours

Difficulty: 1/3

To make this bouquet of crepe paper flowers, you will need:

- Assortment of 10 rolls of crepe paper

Or discover our range of crepe papers

- 20 thread stems with flower 1mm x 50 cm

- Vvinyl glue

- 4 pairs of multi-use scissors

- Cutout template to download, print and cut.

Find all the detailed steps below:

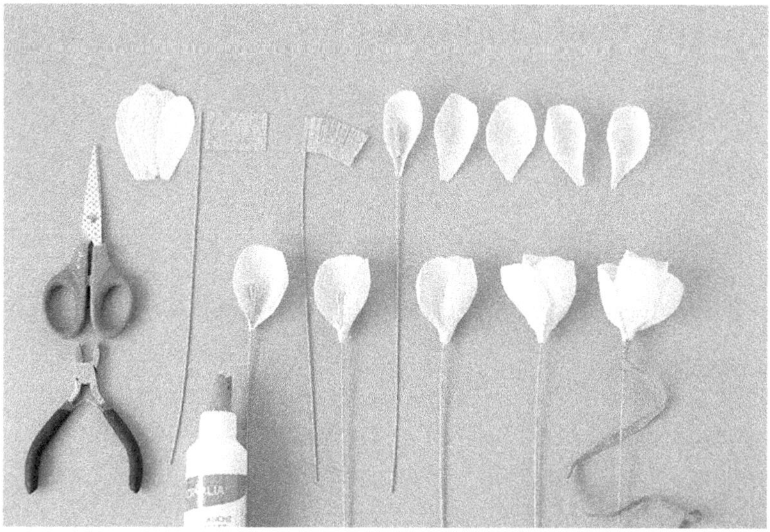

1. Creation of yellow flowers:

Print the template and cut it out on Cricut. Cut 5 petals out of yellow florist crepe paper. Be sure to place the vertical template in the direction of the grooves of the crepe paper. Cut a 2.5 x 5 cm strip of orange florist crepe paper. Bisect a binding wire with a clamp cutting.

Stretch each petal by placing your thumbs in the middle of the petals. Dig with your thumbs apart. The petals become very rounded. Finely notch the orange strip. Paste up the binding wire and winding the paper to form the pistils.

Stick the pistils in the hollow of a first petal. Glue the second petal slightly offset by about 3mm. Glue all the petals until they half cover the first petal. Pinch the basis for refining.

Cut a strip of green crepe paper about 0.5 x 15 cm long. Shoot it. Glue one end to the base of the petals. Apply glue and wrap it tightly around the rod. Leave to dry. Prepare 10 yellow flowers like this.

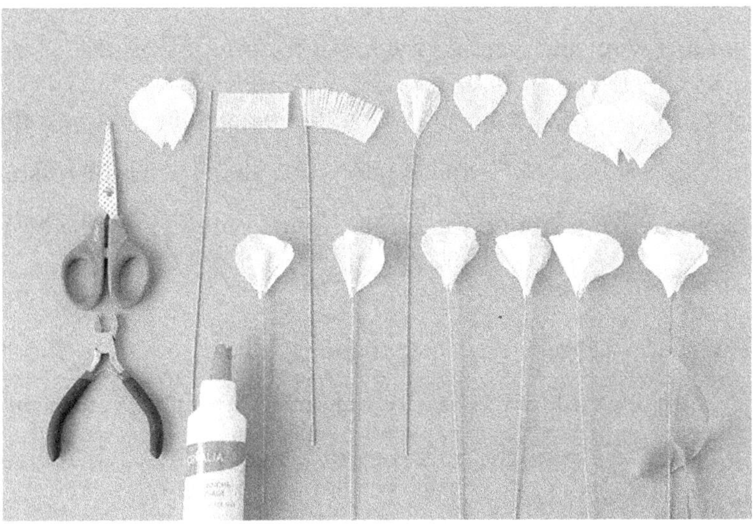

2. Creation of white:

Cut 10 petals out of white florist crepe paper . Be sure to place the vertical template in the direction of the grooves of the crepe paper. Cut a 2.5 x 5 cm strip of yellow florist crepe paper. Cut a wire to be tied in half using wire cutters.

Pinch the top edge of a petal starting from the left and spacing the inches 2 millimeters apart. Stretch the paper. Move your thumbs and repeat the operation every 5 millimeters, to form little ruffles. Do the same for each petal. Place thumbs in the middle of the petals. Dig lightly with your thumbs apart without completely stretching the paper. Finely notch the yellow strip. Stick the top of the binding wire and winding the paper to form the pistils.

Stick the pistils in the hollow of a first petal. Glue the second petal offset by about 5 millimeters. Glue all the petals by rolling the petals to surround the flower several times. Pinch the base to refine it.

Cut a strip of green crepe paper about 0.5 x 15 cm long. Shoot it. Glue one end to the base of the petals. Apply glue and wrap it tightly around the rod. Let dry. Prepare and 10 white flowers.

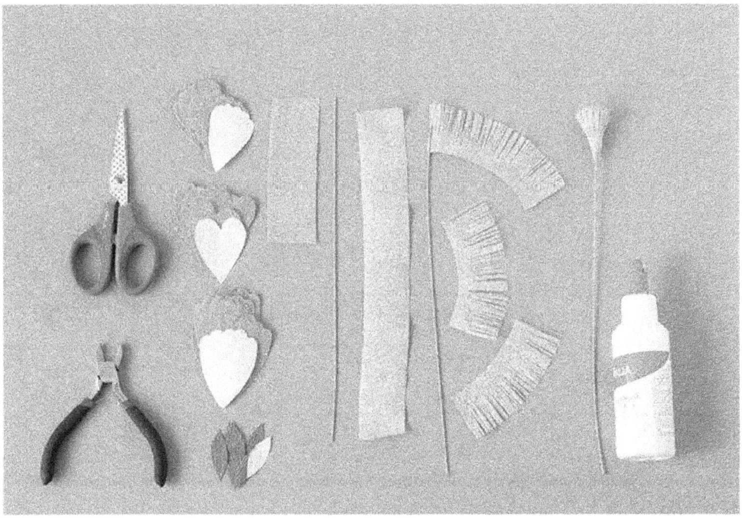

3. Creating peony flowers:

Cut 7 petals of the first template out of bright pink florist crepe paper. Prepare 7 heart-shaped petals and 6 large petals and 5 sepals in green crepe paper . Sure to place the template vertical in the direction of paper grooves crepe.

Cut a 3.5 x 11 cm strip of orange florist crepe paper . Cut into both a binding wire with a clamp cutting.

Stretch the orange strip. Fold it in 3 and cut. Finely notch each orange strip . Glue the first strip to the top of the wire to be bound and roll up the paper to form the pistils. Add the second, then the third strip. Spread the pistils to give them volume. Pinch the base to refine it.

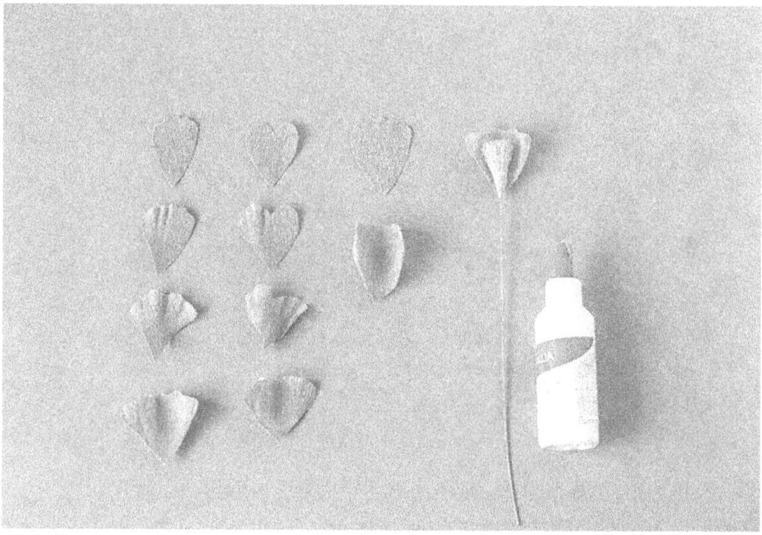

4. Give the form to the petals:

Take the first set of petals. Pinch the top edge of a petal starting from the left and spacing the inches 2 millimeters apart. Stretch the paper. Move your thumbs and repeat the operation every 5 millimeters, to form little ruffles. Do the same for each petal. Place thumbs in the middle of the petals. Widen slightly, keeping inch without fully extend the paper.

Prepare the same way the petals in a heart shape.

For larger petals, stretch them one by one. Place thumbs in the middle of the petals. Dig with your thumbs apart. The petals become very rounded.

Stick the pistils in the hollow of a first petal.

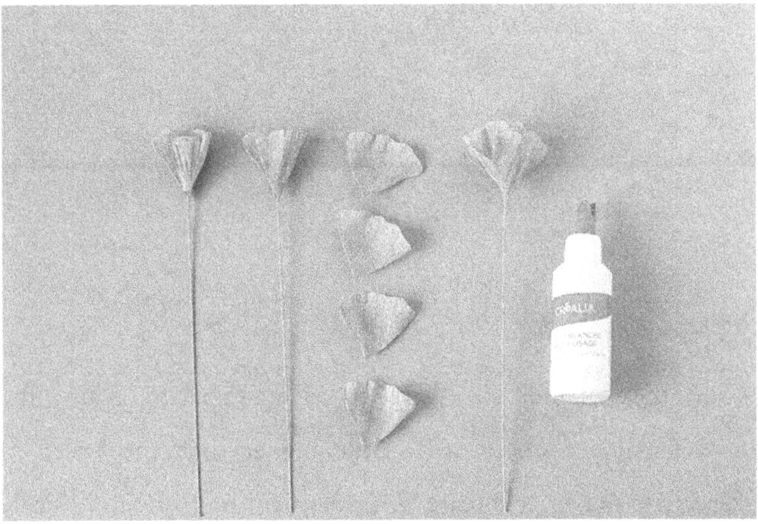

Step 5.

Glue the second petal offset by about 5 millimeters. Glue by wrapping the first 7 petals to surround the flower several times. Pinch the base to refine it.

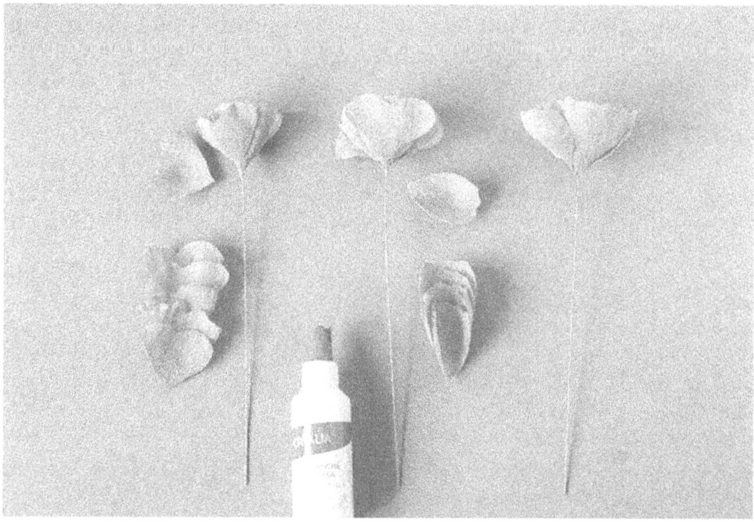

Step 6:

Glue the second set of heart- shaped petals onto the flower. Glue each petal a little higher than the base, on the first petals to create a more garnished effect . Paste wrapping around the petals of the flower.

Finish by gluing the last set of 6 rounded petals, arranging to surround the flower only once.

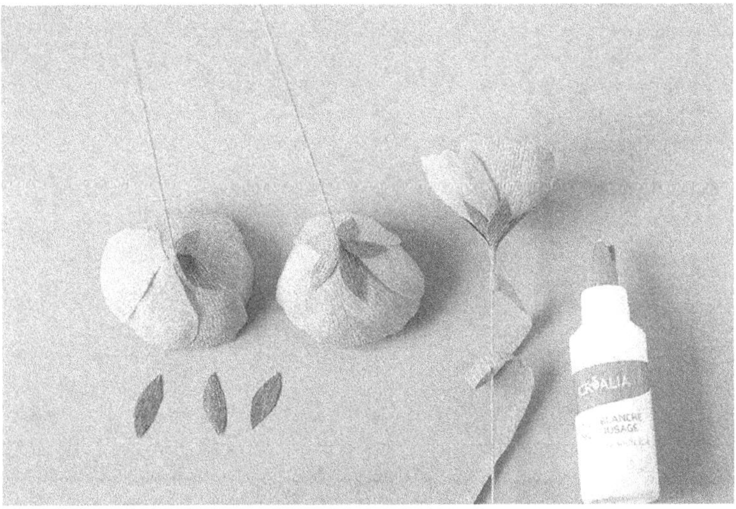

Step 7.

Turn the flower over and glue the sepals starting from the stem to cover the base of the flower. Cut a strip of green crepe paper about 0.4 x 15 cm long . Shoot it. Glue it to the base of the sepals. Apply glue and wrap it tightly around the rod. Let dry. Prepare 5 hot pink peonies and 4 soft pink peonies in this way .

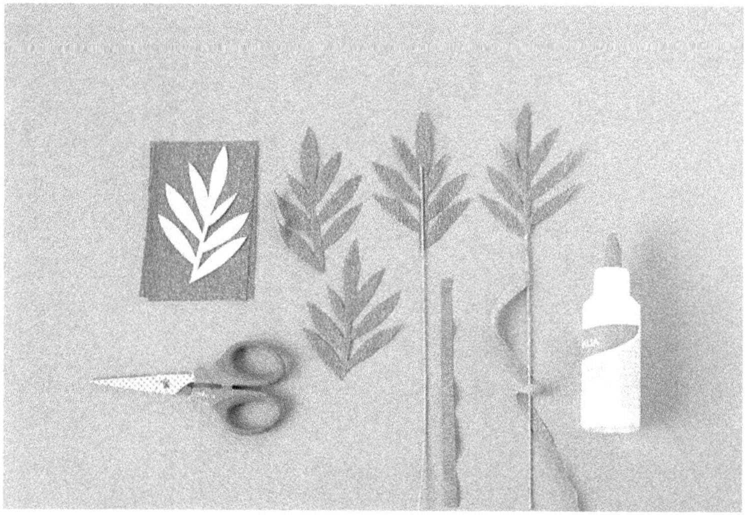

Step 8. The foliage.

Print the template and cut it out using cricut. Cut 10 leaves from green florist crepe paper . Be sure to place the vertical template in the direction of the grooves of the crepe paper. Cut a wire to be tied in half using wire cutters. Paste the wire bonding at the center of the foliage.

Cut a strip of green crepe paper about 0.4 x 15 cm long. Shoot it. The paste to the base of the foliage. Apply glue and wrap it tightly around the rod . Let dry. Prepare 10 green leaves in this way.

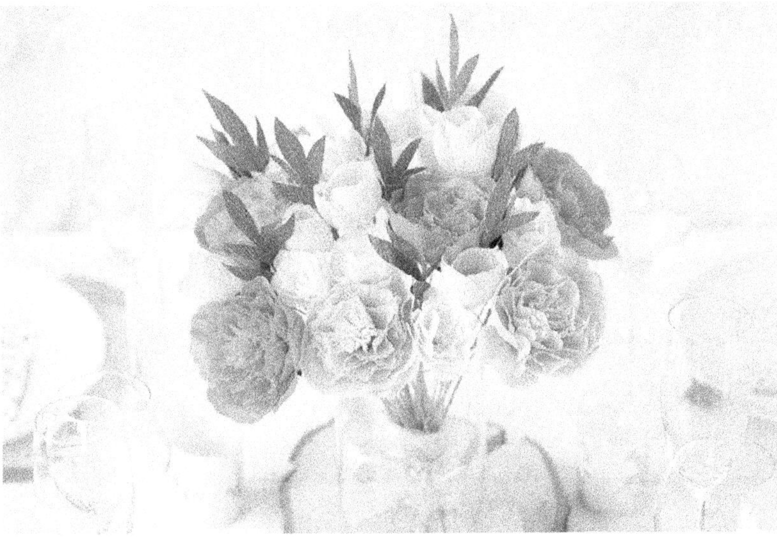

Floral Letter In Watercolor

Time: 60 minutes.

To make your floral letter in watercolor, you will need:

-Cricut Maker

- Box of 12 Aqua pencils

- 3 watercolor brushes

- Watercolor pad 25 x 25 cm

- 200 Double-sided adhesive foam squares - Créalia

- Extra strong double-sided adhesive tape - 6mm x 10m - Créalia

- Template to download and print.

Find all the steps:

STEP 1/9 Print the templates and using the tracing paper, reproduce the letter chosen on the watercolor paper as well as the flowers.

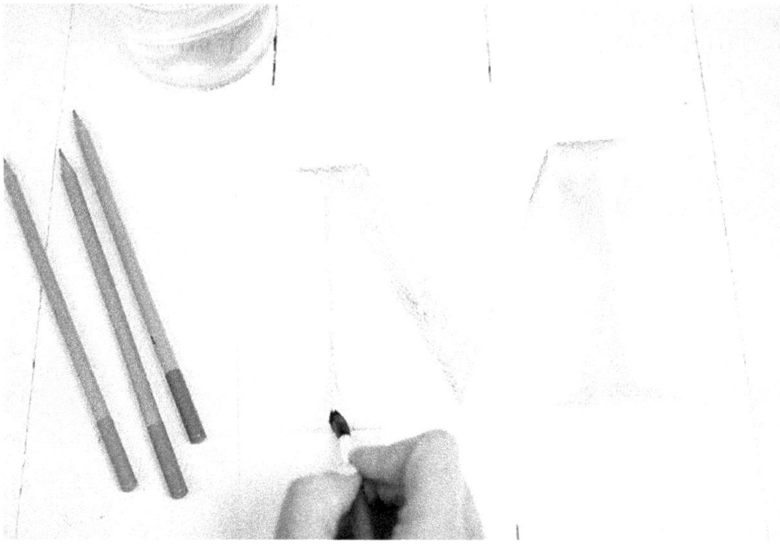

STEP 2/9 Color the letter with watercolor pencils. Make areas darker to create contrast

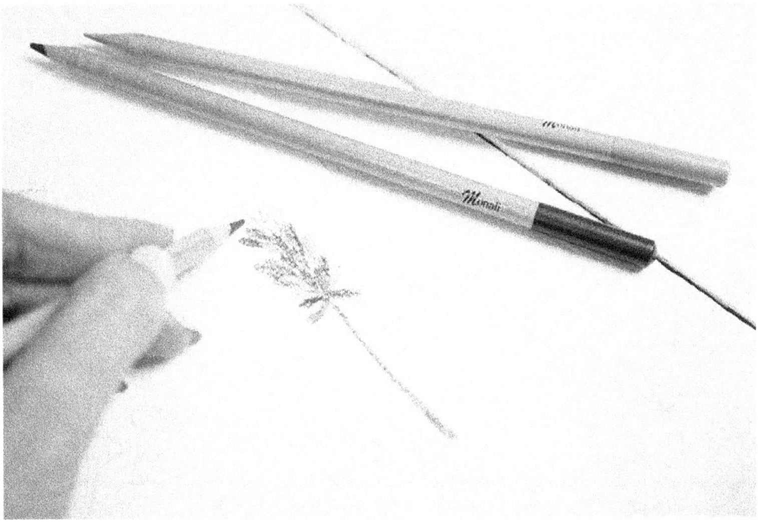

STEP 3/9 Apply water to the entire letter with a watercolor brush

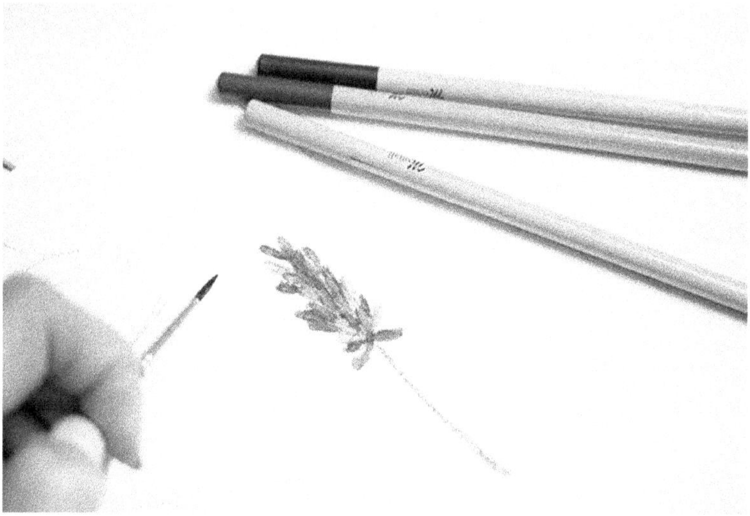

STEP 4/9 Color the plants. For flowers, put different colors on the petals

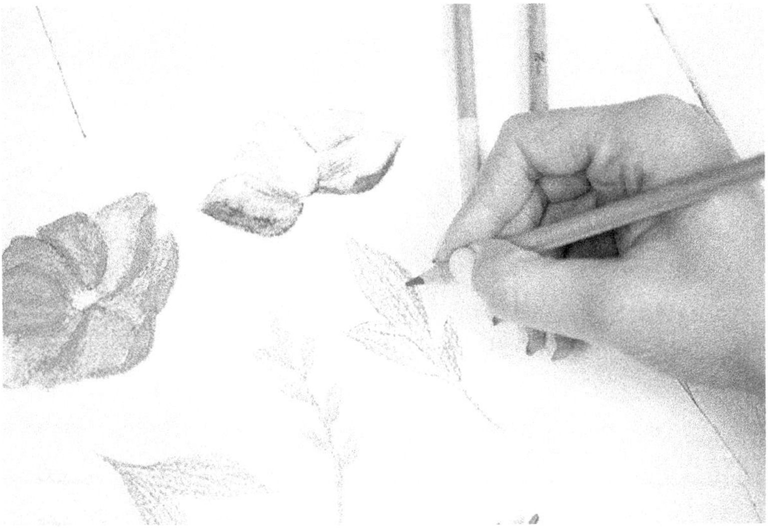

STEP 5/9 With the watercolor brush, apply water and blend the colors together

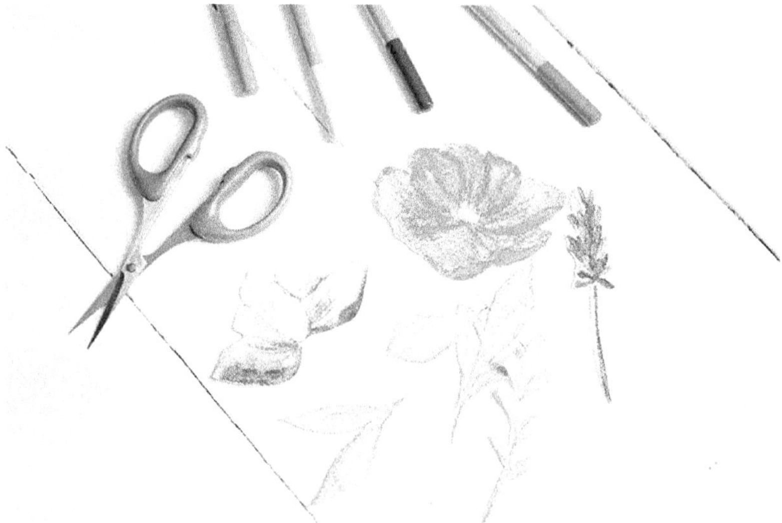

STEP 6/9 For the foliage, apply a first color and add lines of different colors to create nuances

STEP 7/9 Cut out the patterns using Cricut maker.

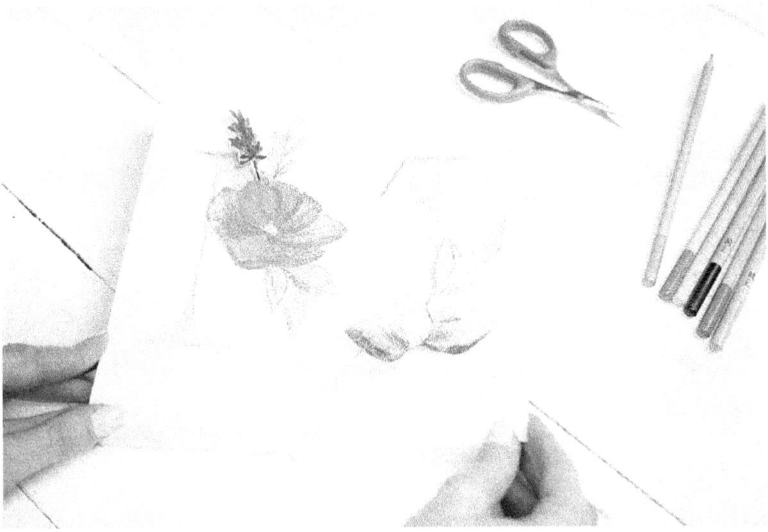

STEP 8/9 Glue the patterns on the letter using the foam squares. Then glue everything on the canvas with double-sided tape.

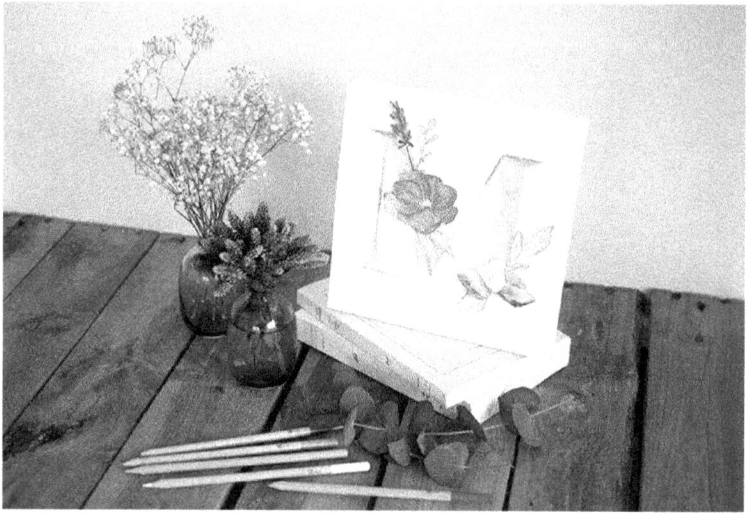

STEP 9/9 Your floral monogram is ready.

Paper Fans

The necessary equipment :

- Circuit Maker
- A4 papers
- Round scalloped perforator 7.5 cm
- Punch Round 3.8cm
- Double-sided
- Mini high temperature glue gun

The stages of the realization:

1. Fold a sheet of A4 paper accordion lengthwise in Cricut maker. Repeat for 2 more sheets of paper.
2. Fold the accordions in half in the middle.
3. Add double-sided tape to the ends

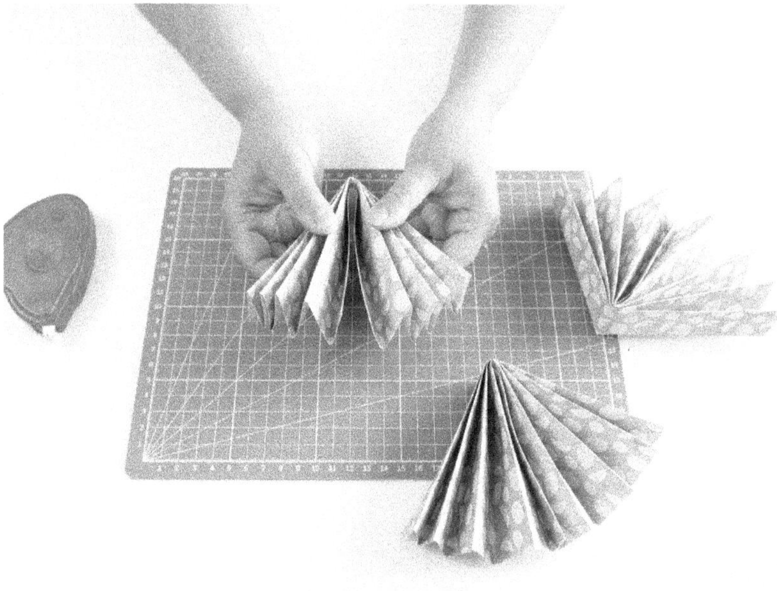

4. Secure the parts together. You must have 3 identical parts.

5. Glue the 3 parts together with double-sided tape to form the pennant.

6. Cut circles using circuit from colored or patterned paper using a scalloped circle hole punch.

7. Glue the circles in the center of each pennant using the glue gun.

8. Repeat the operation with a smaller round hole punch. You can create larger diameter flags by gluing 2 A4 sheets together in the longest part of the paper beforehand to form A3 paper.

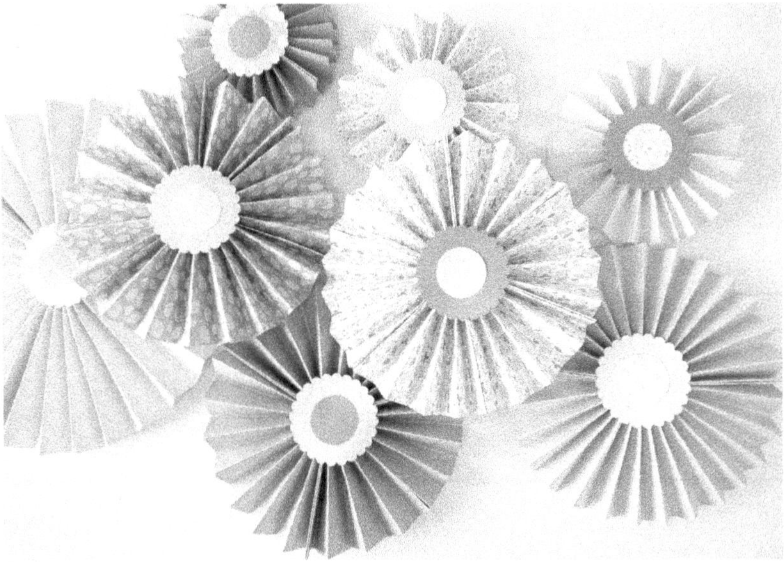

9. Create several fans by varying sizes to decorate your party atmosphere.

Thankyou Box

- The Cricut Machine

- Color papers

- Glue

- Removable golden vinyl

- Gold Marker

- The template

- The typos used are Courrier new and Adalaide (the latter is from Cricut)

- For those who can log into Cricut, here is the Design Space project link .

Discover all the steps below:

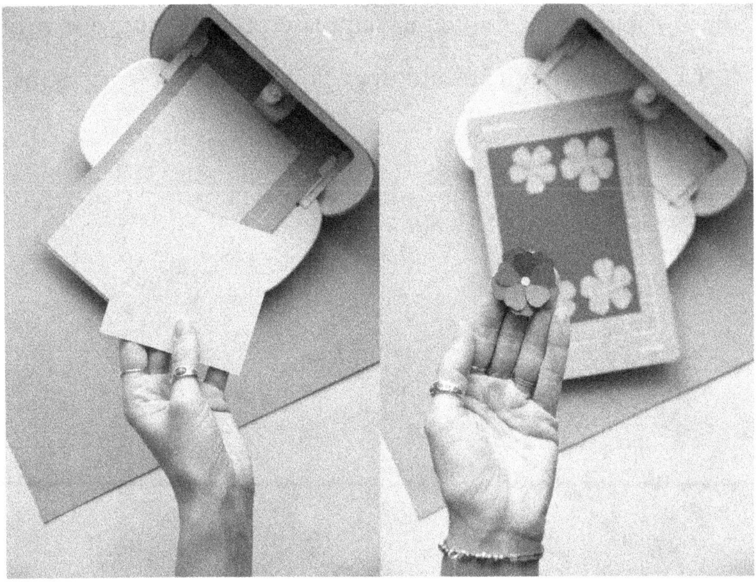

Step 1 / Using your application prepare the cutting of your paper templates for your box, as well as the paper decorations (ex: foliage / flowers / hearts).

Step 1 BIS / Using your application prepare the cutting of your paper templates for your box, as well as the paper decorations (ex: leaves / flowers / hearts).

Step 2 / Prepare the cutting of your heart stickers with your SMART VINYL REMOVABLE Gold paper which you will use to close your box.

Step 3 / Now that the paper templates are cut out, use your GOLD marker to create and draw your texts. You can choose to write whatever you want.

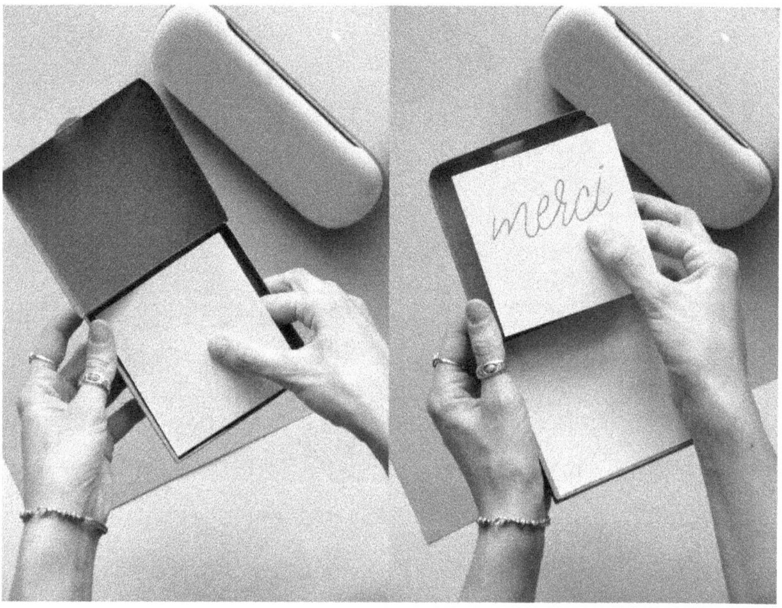

Step 4 / It's time to stick your papers on your cardboard box. The "Thank you" paper is to be placed inside the box on the upper part. Also place your plain pink paper template at the bottom of your box.

Step 4 bis / Now stick your paper with your text “Just for you” on the outside of the box.

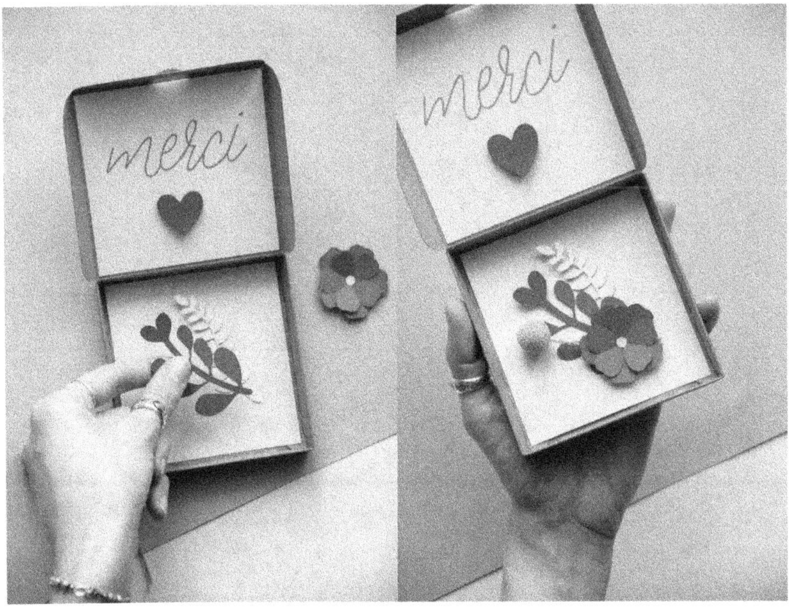

Step 5 / Come and create your floral arrangement inside your box using strong glue, I decided to add a real craspedia to it so that I don't just have paper. If not, you can add a branch of eucalyptus, or olive tree.

Step 6 / Once your interior decoration is finished, you can now close your box and seal it with your golden heart stickers. All you have to do is offer them.

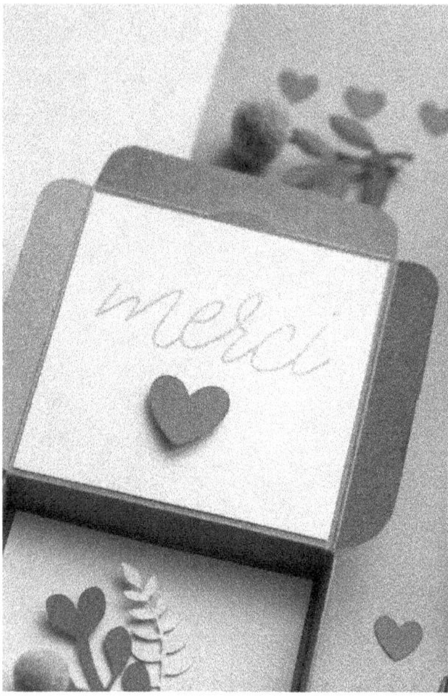
merci
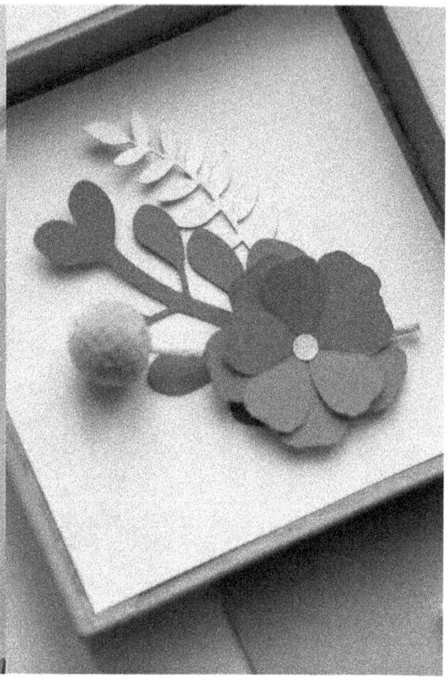

Cricut Project Procedure

Before you begin, download the desktop version of Cricut Design Space.

In the application you can load images of various types: .jpg, .gif, .bmp, .svg or .dxf.

The non-vector images, if they are in a single color, we will have no problem when editing them to cut; if it is a png, nothing should be done, the program automatically detects the outline, but if it is a .jpg, we will have to remove everything that is background.

It is very simple when what we want to cut is a single color, since in that case, with the magic wand we would eliminate the background and READY TO CUT! But what do we do when the image we want to make is in various colors? In this case, we will have to create several files to be able to separate them and it is a somewhat more complex process. But let's not be alarmed, in this post we are going to make a multi-color image step by step to see the process that we should follow with a .jpg image.

OPEN NEW PROJECT AND LOAD IMAGE

- This is the main Design Space window when you open it. To start we select New project
- When we click on New project, our workspace opens , there we select Upload
- This screen will open where it tells us the types of files that can be uploaded, we, as we said at the beginning of this post, we are going to upload a JPG image . To load the image we can search for it on our PC or drag it into the window that appears.

IMAGE EDIT: REMOVE BACKGROUND AND SEPARATE COLORS

- Once we have our image loaded, we select its complexity, as it is an image with a lot of color and so that it detects all the detail, we select the Complex mode. If the image were a silhouette or two or three colors, we could select the Simple mode.
- To start editing our image, we select the magic wand , with it we can erase with a single click a mass of the same color, in this case, we have eliminated the entire background at once
- If we select the preview button, we can see the contour that it detects to be able to crop. As you can see, we

would do the whole drawing in a single cut, so we need to separate the colors.

- With the help of the eraser, we can eliminate the elements that we do not want to cut, in this step, we are making the black layer first. You have to check from time to time with the option "Preview" that we do not have any element that we do not want.
- When we have our finished color layer we select Continue, in the next window we will get two types of saving modes: To print and cut (if we want to print the complete drawing and then cut only the silhouette) or as a Cut Image, we will we will save like this since we will use it to make a project with textile vinyl.
- Then we repeat the whole process of uploading the image and editing it with all the colors we want.
- Once we have all of them uploaded, we select them and click Insert Images, to be able to load them in our workspace.

EDITING THE IMAGE ON THE WORKTABLE

- When we have our files loaded in the workspace, so that when cutting, we automatically have it separated by colors, we will assign a color to each of the layers.

- And we already have our project ready to cut! If the work is for textiles and has text, you have to remember to mirror it, so that when ironing it is legible.

CPSIA information can be obtained
at www.ICGtesting.com
Printed in the USA
LVHW020025301120
672966LV00023B/263

9 781513 672168